The Imam, the Pasha and the Englishman

MICHAEL CRAWFORD

The Imam, the Pasha and the Englishman

The Ordeal of ʿAbd Allah ibn Saʿud, Cairo 1818

Arabian Publishing

The Imam, the Pasha and the Englishman
The Ordeal of 'Abd Allah ibn Sa'ud, Cairo 1818
by Michael Crawford

Produced and published in 2024 by
Arabian Publishing Ltd
a division of Medina Publishing Ltd
www.medinapublishing.com

Medina Publishing   Arabian Publishing

Editor: William Facey

Design and digital artwork: Medina Publishing Ltd

Printed by Interak in Poland

A catalogue record for this publication is available from the British Library

ISBN: 978-1-911487-98-2

To Georgia

CONTENTS

List of illustrations and maps

Illustrations

Maps

The 1816–18 invasion route through the Hijaz and Najd to al-Dir'iyya

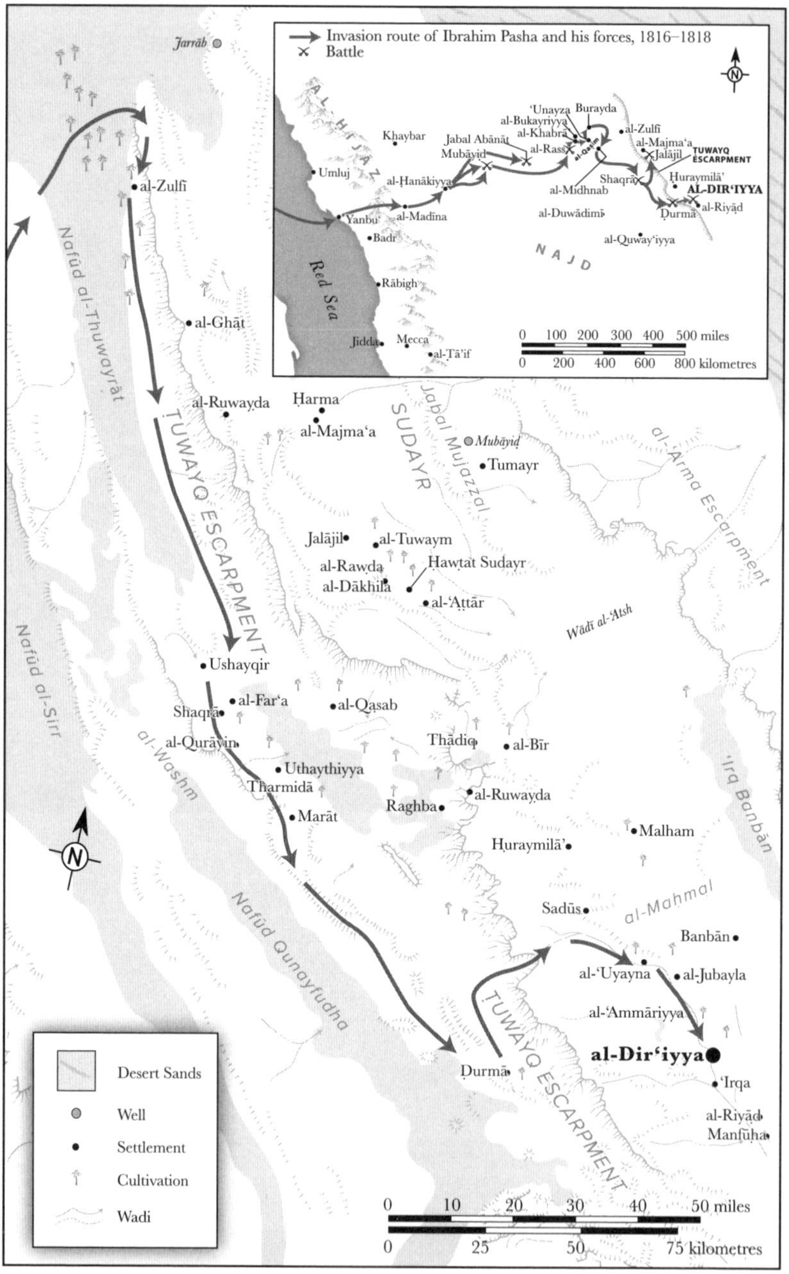

Imam 'Abd Allāh's route from al-Dir'iyya to Istanbul, 1818

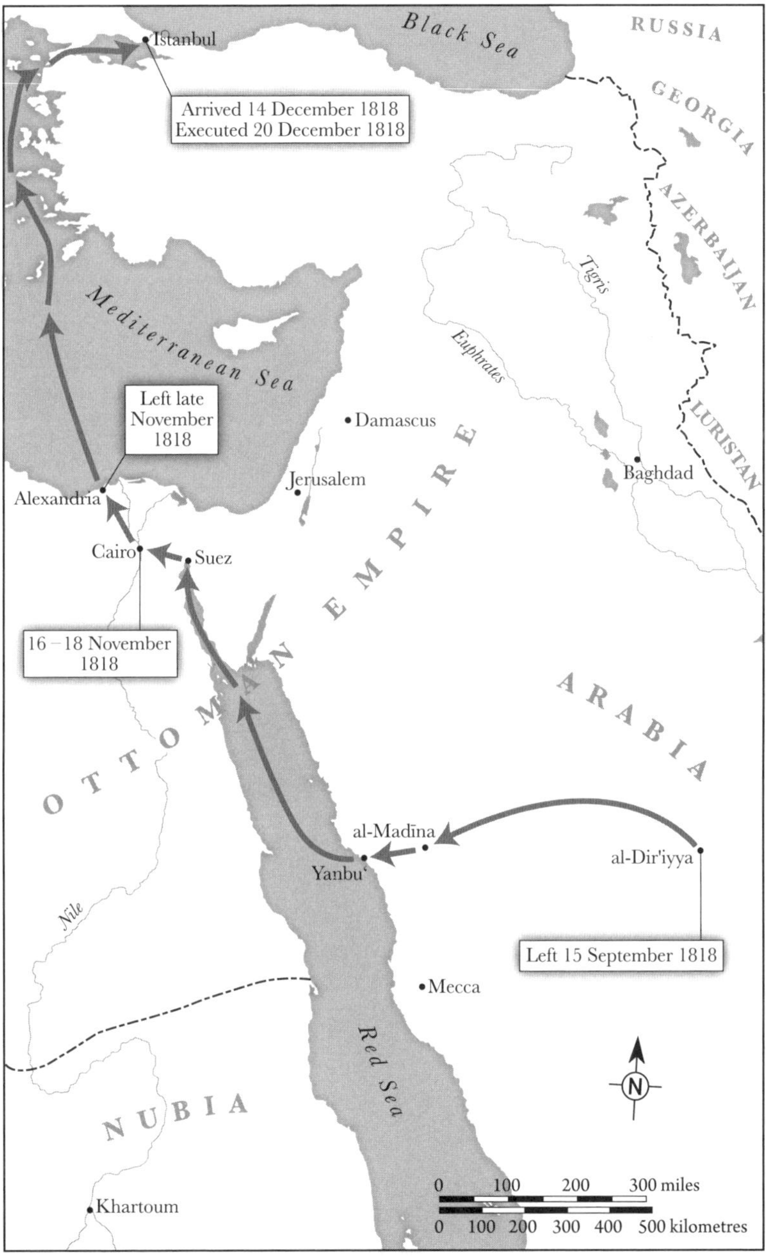

BOWES WRIGHT'S TRAVELS IN THE EASTERN MEDITERRANEAN, 1818–19

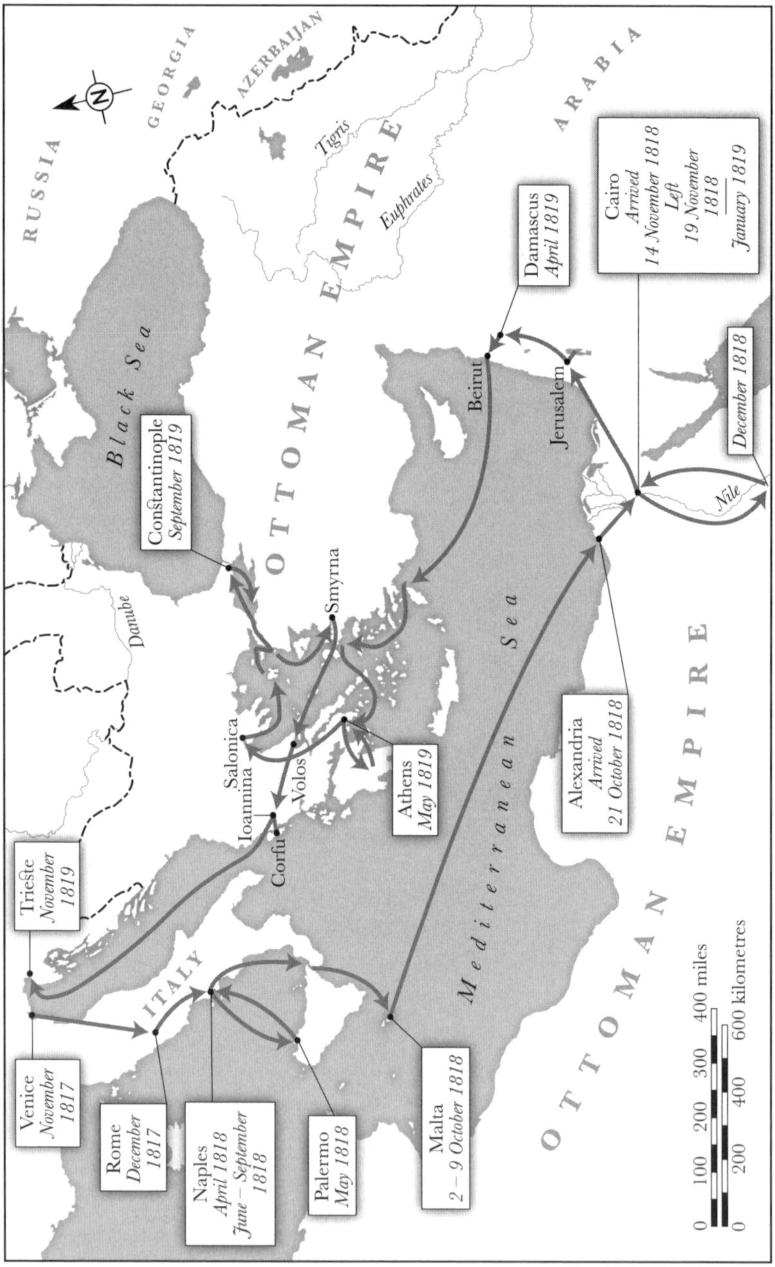

Preface

The past is not static. The ground on which the present rests is constantly shifting. The historian's task is to reinvestigate and reinterpret the foundations of our world, and to challenge our understanding of them in the light of fresh evidence, insights or ways of thinking, as they emerge. Seeking to impose an official or ideological straitjacket on this process is an arbitrary exercise, one that is, ultimately, both futile and damaging. If the writing of history is to prosper and we are to understand better why our world is as it is, it is vital we acknowledge and safeguard the role in historiography of pluralism in thought and approach.

Sa'ūdi Arabia has never espoused pluralism in either religion or politics. In recent decades, it has devoted much effort to curating the historical and religious record, seeing it as integral to its present-day image. Most observers were taken aback by the sudden issue, in January 2022, of a royal order, specifying in which year the current state's forerunner was founded in the early 18th century. Conventionally, this is known as the First Sa'ūdi State — even if, through most of that century, it was a minor principality in central Arabia that hardly met modern criteria for a state. Local chronicles agree that this entity gained dramatic expansionary impetus after the sealing of an alliance in 1744 between the petty Āl Sa'ūd dynasty, which ruled the settlement of al-Dir'iyya and its environs, and the radical Wahhābi religious movement. Traditionally, that date has been accepted as marking the launch of the original 'state'.

By laying down that the First Sa'ūdi State was instead founded in 1727, before the creation of the Wahhābi movement, the royal fiat seeks to belittle, or even airbrush from the official narrative, the crucial part played by Wahhābism, and its activist founder Ibn 'Abd al-Wahhāb, in the creation and remarkable achievements of the First Sa'ūdi State. It remains to be seen how far this doctrine, driven by today's politics and a desire to rebrand the state, will have a chilling impact on the writing of 18th and 19th century history by new generations of Sa'ūdi scholars. Available textual evidence from that era, derived almost exclusively from Wahhābi sources, leaves little scope for serious revisionist scholarship.

This book focuses, not on the start of the First Sa'ūdi State, but on its end. It describes the impact of military defeat on the Sa'ūdi dynasty and on the Wahhābi movement, which continued to operate in tandem to the last. It has been inspired by a previously unidentified English source, who attended one of the most dramatic scenes in the state's career. The parabola of expansion, triumph and disaster that marked the Sa'ūdi and Wahhābi experience in the first two decades of the 19th century found its symbolic end in an encounter between the vanquished Sa'ūdi leader and his Ottoman nemesis in Cairo in late 1818. The occasion was witnessed by an Englishman. It is his account that underpins this study. It is rare to come across a new European source on the early Wahhābis.

British official material bearing on Sa'ūdi history has long been readily available, some of it handily presented in the relevant Cambridge Archive Edition published in 2013.[1] Foreign official records on the First Sa'ūdi State are supplemented by the published memoirs or accounts of contemporary European officials based in Ottoman lands, and by the travelogues of those touched by Wahhābi activities on the fringes of Arabia. In the early 19th century, a new category of hardy European travellers became prominent in the region. They made adventurous journeys for pleasure or in pursuit of private ambitions, not for official or business purposes. They faced considerable hazards, especially the ubiquitous plague. It is salutary to be reminded by their correspondence, as well as local chronicles, how far 'the plague' (a generic label for a range of sicknesses) hovered like a dark shadow over their everyday existences and future plans. It is one of these enterprising travellers, a Fellow of Jesus College, Cambridge, with a knack for being in the right place at the right time, who casts a fresh light on the final act of the First Sa'ūdi State. He also gives us the only first-hand physical description we have of an early Sa'ūdi ruler by someone who met him.

---

[1] Burdett, ed., *The Expansion of Wahhabi Power in Arabia 1798–1932* (8 vols).

John Bowes Wright (1779–1836), a well-connected traveller and inveterate correspondent, offers new and valuable insights on the transit of the Saʿūdi ruler through Cairo on his last journey to execution. His account first came to public notice in 1999, when the letter recording this happenstance was mentioned briefly in the ASTENE bulletin.[2] This letter forms part of a still unpublished archive of correspondence between Bowes Wright and his close friend Joseph Lamb (1781–1859), passed down through the latter's descendants and still in the possession of the Lamb family today.[3] I am grateful to Lady (Penny) Marland, sole literary legatee of her late father Richard Lamb Snr, for access to this correspondence and for permission to quote excerpts and to publish in full the letter of 18 November 1818 from Cairo.

This study began life as a short article published in 2017 under the long title ' 'Abd Allāh Al Saʿūd and Muḥammad ʿAlī Pasha: The Theatre of Victory, the Prophet's Treasures, and the Visiting Whig, Cairo 1818'.[4] My co-author was William Facey, who first alerted me to Bowes Wright's encounter with Muḥammad ʿAlī Pasha and Imam 'Abd Allāh in Cairo, and was kind enough to share access to the relevant correspondence. When the article developed into a longer study, he exchanged co-authorship for the role of editor. I am grateful to both him and Peter Harrigan, director of Arabian Publishing, for their comments, assistance and support with this work. I also wish to thank that generous scholar Dr. Saud al-Sarhan for giving me access to various relevant Arabic sources and for his advice on aspects of the text.

I also express my gratitude to Jeff Eamon, Sherif Dhaimish and Alexandra Lawson, all of Arabian Publishing, for their help with the text, illustrations and maps. My son-in-law Arnaud Chougny kindly assisted with the time-ravaged image of Captain Ford's drawing of Cairo. Finally, I should record my thanks to Martin Lubikowski of ML Design, who drew the maps.

---

[2] Manley 1999: 19.

[3] These letters are distinct from the Lamb Family Papers held by the Northumberland Archives.

[4] Formal acknowledgement: this book is derived in part from this article published in the *Journal of Arabian Studies* 7 (1) (April 2017) (© Taylor & Francis), pp. 44–62, available online: https://www.tandfonline.com/doi/full/10.1080/21534764.2017.1304509. See Crawford and Facey 2017.

The Bowes Wright letters

All the letters made available to me have been previously transcribed into typed versions, on which I have relied, by the late Richard Lamb Snr., who envisaged their publication in their entirety. In line with a common practice of the time, Bowes Wright headed each letter with a Roman numeral so that the recipient would know if one had gone missing. Unfortunately, this system of logging sometimes becomes confused, so I have not used these numerals in referring to individual letters. All letters mentioned belong to the Bowes Wright/Lamb series, unless otherwise indicated. Bowes Wright's letter of 18 November 1818 from Cairo is set out in full in the appendix.

Wahhābism

I have used the terms 'Wahhābi' and 'Wahhābism' with neutral intent. Those who subscribe to Ibn 'Abd al-Wahhāb's interpretation of Islam today regard these labels as derogatory. They call themselves 'Salafis', submerging their identity in a much wider and more diverse religious trend. In the period covered by this book, adherents of Ibn 'Abd al-Wahhāb's doctrines identified themselves as '*muwaḥḥidūn*' (practitioners of *tawḥīd* or oneness of God) or simply 'the Muslims'. For other Muslims and Europeans, they were the Wahhābis and their imam was often called 'the Wahhābi'. One exiled Wahhābi, who had fought for the Sa'ūdis against the invading Ottomans, even wrote in 1818 of 'the Wahhābis'.[5] Since this Wahhābi label was used at the time, has been widely employed since, and is generally recognised today, I have adopted it in this book.

Transliteration from Arabic, and place names

I have followed current academic practice with this, including diacritics, in line with the system used by the *International Journal of Middle East Studies* (IJMES). In the case of place names that have a widely accepted spelling in English (e.g. Cairo, Hijaz, Mecca), I have adopted those in the text, and have avoided diacritics with Arabic terms or titles commonly used in English (such as hajj, imam, pasha, sultan). Broadly, I have also followed

5 Al-Bassām 2010: e.g. 54, 80.

the IJMES system with Ottoman Turkish names and titles and with Turkish place names.

Where appropriate, I have sometimes called the Ottoman capital 'Constantinople', since this is how Bowes Wright and contemporary British officialdom and press referred to it. This sounds quaint to modern ears, but then Saʻūdis of the time often named it al-Rūm, i.e. Byzantium. Elsewhere in the text, the city is rendered 'Istanbul'.

Dates

I have given all dates in the Gregorian calendar. Some of the Arabic sources give only an Islamic calendar (Hijri) year for an event. Where it is unclear in which Gregorian year that event fell, I have rendered the relevant date in the format 1814/15. I have made the conversion using *http://www.muslimphilosophy.com/ip/hijri.htm*.

Michael Crawford
Oxfordshire 2024

CHAPTER 1

Victor and Vanquished

Triumphant pasha and dispossessed imam

In late 1818 Muḥammad 'Alī Pasha (1770–1849), Ottoman governor of Egypt, was on an upward trajectory, poised to exploit his military triumph over the Wahhābis to extend his control and influence into Arabia and the Levant, as well as found a dynasty in Cairo. His doomed captive, who had inherited from his father the burden of defending Sa'ūdi domains, could take no comfort from contemplating past or future. He had just witnessed Muḥammad 'Alī's soldier son, Ibrāhīm Pasha (1789–1848), destroy his Islamic empire and capital. Now he was en route to Istanbul, his life in the hands of the vengeful Ottomans, who were still smarting at being designated unbelievers (*kuffār*) by hard-line Wahhābi clerics.

The journey of Sa'ūdi Imam 'Abd Allāh ibn Sa'ūd from his occupied capital in Central Arabia to certain death in Istanbul in late 1818 came as a grim postscript to the spectacular career of the First Sa'ūdi State. With his execution, the first Islamic state of pre-modern times passed into history. His transit through Cairo coincided with the culmination of victory celebrations staged by Muḥammad 'Alī to mark his triumph. It also heralded the point at which the pasha began to pursue his regional ambitions beyond Sudan and Arabia.

For the pasha's notional sovereign, Ottoman Sultan Maḥmūd II (1785–1839), the doomed imam's beheading in Istanbul also represented a crucial inflection point. The public act of revenge helped expunge the religious and regional shame inflicted on the Ottomans and their sultan by the Wahhābi occupation of the Hijaz and their exclusion from the

Holy Cities, of which the sultan was formally guardian and protector. The triumph of arms belonged to Maḥmūd's governor, but the pasha's expedition into Arabia to subdue the Wahhābis had been at the sultan's instruction. Maḥmūd was determined, even desperate, to exploit a rare victory to consolidate his domestic rule and project himself regionally as a powerful monarch with a long reach. This required him to humiliate as well as execute his defeated adversary.

The final travails of Imam ʿAbd Allāh form an episode to which 19th- and early 20th-century Saʿūdi chroniclers and *ʿulamāʾ* (clerics) chose to give only cursory attention.[1] Nor have modern Saʿūdi historians shown greater interest. Perhaps unfairly, this stolid Wahhābi leader has historically carried much of the blame for the disaster that befell his people. He has been judged unequal to the task of defending his country. One Arabian historian commented succinctly: "He was a brave man but not much of a politician."[2] It is telling that the key Saʿūdi chronicler ʿUthmān ibn Bishr (d. 1873/4) gives him a curt obituary, in contrast to the pages of effusive encomia devoted to preceding Saʿūdi leaders.[3]

ʿAbd Allāh had succeeded his politically astute and extravagant father Saʿūd (b. 1751/2) on the latter's death in May 1814, possibly after suppressing a challenge from his brother Fayṣal (d. 1818)[4] or uncle ʿAbd Allāh (d. 1818), the latter supported by some Wahhābi clerics.[5] Family frictions aside, political and military circumstances had turned against the Saʿūdis. Imam Saʿūd's territorial expansionism and aggressive approach

---

[1] Al-Fākhirī (d. 1860) 1999: 182; Ibn Bishr 1982–83 i: 421–2; Ibn ʿĪsā (d. 1925) 1999: 107–08. We do not know in which year ʿAbd Allāh was born.

[2] Al-Rashīd (d. 1913) 1966: 29. Burckhardt comments on ʿAbd Allāh's lack of touch in managing the tribes (1831 ii: 288). In a sustained indictment, Mengin accuses him of vengefulness, parsimony, poor judgment, failure to listen to advice, and poor military strategy and tactics (1823 ii: 141–3). See also ibid. ii: 48.

[3] See Ibn Bishr 1982–83 i: 422; ii: 17.

[4] As suggested by Shaykh ʿAbd al-Raḥmān Āl al-Shaykh (d. 1869) 2005: 116–17. He was one of the *qāḍīs* of al-Dirʿiyya under Imams Saʿūd and ʿAbd Allāh (Ibn Bishr 1982–83 i: 363, 423).

[5] Burckhardt 1831 ii: 288. The Ottomans too picked up stories of disputes between Saʿūd's sons (Mawjānī 2014: 395, giving the Arabic translated text of a letter from Aḥmad Bazmī to Muḥammad Najīb of 26 June 1814). Neither of chroniclers Ibn Bishr (1982–83 i: 365) or al-Fākhirī (1999: 175) mentions rivals for the imamate. ʿAbd Allāh ibn Saʿūd was already designated crown prince (*walī al-ʿahd*). In the Hijaz, when news came of Saʿūd's death, he received immediate allegiance (Ibn Bishr 1982–83 i: 368).

to Ottoman regional capitals had brought Ottoman retribution through the agency of Muḥammad ʿAlī Pasha. The pasha was a man of formidable experience and ambition, familiar with contemporary warfare, and with access to reserves of money, materiel and manpower that Imam ʿAbd Allāh could not match. Confronted by his invading forces, ʿAbd Allāh struggled resolutely against the odds and paid the price for his father's overreach and high-handedness. His understated style contrasted with his father's love of splendour and finery.[6] He was more of a soldier: "With respect to courage and skill in war, his reputation exceeded that of his father."[7] His final encounters with his victors in Cairo and Istanbul were to the credit of his character and fortitude. They also marked a humiliating denouement for the first incarnation of the Wahhābi movement – one that later generations of Wahhābis have preferred to gloss over.

A meeting of contrasting worlds

Contemporary accounts of the interplay between the Saʿūdi imam, Muḥammad ʿAlī Pasha, and Sultan Maḥmūd throw an interesting light on these three leading protagonists in the Ottoman–Wahhābi conflict and on their differing political and religious cultures. This study focuses primarily on the direct encounter between the imam and the pasha, the former's treatment by the Sublime Porte, and the sultan's relationship with Muḥammad ʿAlī. Sultan Maḥmūd took a keen personal interest in the imam's fate and observed his arraignment from a distance, but he does not seem to have met him in person. As the supreme political and religious authority in Istanbul, he kept himself resolutely in the background during this theatrical proceeding, while making the most of his own staged appearance.

The account presented here draws on the hitherto unpublished report of an incidental English witness, John Bowes Wright, to the imam's short transit in Cairo. He attended ʿAbd Allāh's session with Muḥammad ʿAlī, watched his surrender to his nemesis of the Prophet's treasures in his

6 For a description of a busy and prosperous al-Dirʿiyya at the height of Saʿūd's reign, see Ibn Bishr 1982–83 i: 44.

7 Burckhardt 1831 ii: 288. Ibn Bishr comments that he was more stalwart in standing up to the enemy than his father (1982–83 i: 422). There was sometimes a question mark placed over Saʿūd's bravery in battle (Lorimer 1915 i (Pt. 1B): 1062–3).

possession, and offers descriptions of the two men, including the only pen-portrait we have of the imam by someone who met him. In describing his experiences, the Englishman reveals his own set of assumptions, some reflecting those of his British and Ottoman hosts in Cairo, others his personal Whiggish political and cultural outlook.

The meeting between pasha and imam in mid-November 1818 marked the symbolic conclusion to a long attritional conflict with heavy religious overtones. The two men belonged to contrasting regional cultures. One was a self-made warlord from the Aegean port of Kavala in eastern Macedonia, an Ottoman culturally with a transnational outlook and conventional attitude to religion that he did not let interfere with his skilful practice of *realpolitik*. His tolerance of other creeds struck Western visitors forcefully, and attracted criticism from traditionalist local elements hostile to some of his domestic reforms. Le Comte de Forbin (1779–1841), the head of an official French mission who called on the pasha several times in Alexandria in early 1818, observed appreciatively: "Ce prince est fort tolérant en matière de religion ; il savoure publiquement et sans scrupule les vins de Chyrâz, de Chypre et de Bordeaux."[8] The pasha had a broad perspective on the wider world and was impressively well informed on political, military and commercial developments around the Mediterranean.

Appointed governor (*wālī*) by the Ottomans in July 1805, a few months after a failed attempt by them to make him *wālī* in unhealthy Jidda, a graveyard of Ottoman governors,[9] Muḥammad ʿAlī was working to gain guaranteed security of tenure in Cairo and to found a ruling house. Whether from the outset he aimed to achieve autonomy or independence of Istanbul is a moot point. His attitude to the Ottomans seems to have been ambivalent and conflicted.[10] His desire to serve the sultan, and be deemed by him to have done so admirably, was mixed with an urge to escape the burdens and constraints imposed on him by the Sublime Porte. His handling of the European powers reflected a similarly complex blend of fear, admiration, need, and desire for recognition. A man of strategic

---

[8] De Forbin 1819: 302–3: "This prince is remarkably tolerant in regard to religion; he enjoys, publicly and shamelessly, the wines of Shiraz, Cyprus and Bordeaux."

[9] Al-Jabartī 1958–67 vi: 217, 231; Ṣābān 2004: 197.

[10] As discussed by Fahmy 2002: 22–5.

vision, he was a skilled political tactician and accomplished manipulator, with a well-deserved reputation for ruthlessness, subtlety, and treachery. Until shortly before he met Imam ʻAbd Allāh, he was illiterate.

The imam,[11] heir to a freshly minted dynasty now at risk of being eliminated, was the product of small-town Central Arabia, hostile to the Ottomans, and a carefully trained champion of the exclusivist Wahhābi creed, which treated most co-religionists as non-Muslim. He had received a religious education, as all Saʻūdi leaders did, and was known as a strong upholder of the Sharīʻa and regime of godliness, with a high regard for Wahhābi clerics (*ʻulamāʼ*).[12] He had spent his whole career in the Arabian Peninsula within a closed political and religious system. His window on regional developments was narrow, his outlook uncomplicated, and his personal style, at least as reflected in correspondence with Muḥammad ʻAlī in Cairo and the British in the Gulf, straightforward and direct. He would probably never have met a Christian or Jew before arriving in Cairo.

That John Bowes Wright, Fellow of Jesus College, Cambridge and an English Whig, should have been introduced to Imam ʻAbd Allāh in Cairo and witnessed his encounter with the pasha – as well as the return of the treasures, which had great symbolic value for the Ottomans but had been treated in a casually utilitarian fashion by the Wahhābis – makes the occasion all the more remarkable. Tourists and travellers can find themselves inadvertently witnessing momentous events, sometimes without appreciating their contemporary or potential historical significance. This was not true of Bowes Wright on this or other occasions during a long career of travelling. This enthusiastic and perceptive correspondent was both inquisitive and politically attuned, and enjoyed easy access to influential figures in London and Paris, and when on the road. He well recognised and appreciated the import of events he experienced at first hand. The happenstance in Cairo was no exception, although his travel plans left him with little opportunity to reflect on it directly afterwards in his letter home.

---

[11] The term *imam*, which has various meanings in Islam, signifies here the political and religious leader of the Saʻūdi state. The title *imām al-muslimīn* was first assumed by ʻAbd Allāh's father, Saʻūd, on or soon after his accession in November 1803.

[12] Ibn Bishr 1982–83 i: 422.

Wahhābism as understood by an English traveller

The meeting between the imam and the pasha that Bowes Wright and an English companion or companions witnessed was the only one between the two foes. All those present at the meeting in the palace set in fragrant gardens at Shubrā – even the English visitors – recognised that, once in Istanbul, 'Abd Allāh faced Ottoman interrogation and execution. Showing how readily he had imbibed prevailing Cairene views of Wahhābi irreligion, Bowes Wright observed: "It is generally believed ['Abd Allāh] will lose his head on his arrival, not only as having been so formidable a rebel to the state, but as having even threatened with absolute destruction the holy Mussulman Faith."[13] Here he echoed a longstanding British view in Egypt that the Wahhābis were "the enemies of the Mahometan faith".[14] Such confusion over the nature of Wahhābi beliefs still prevailed in Western capitals, a result of the controversy that had stalked the Wahhābi movement from its inception.[15]

The Wahhābis saw themselves as restoring Islam to its original purity by stripping out accretions and distortions of belief and practice that had accumulated since the first generations of Muslims.[16] But their uncompromising and unforgiving ideological campaign and rigorous enforcement of their regime of godliness aroused immediate and intense opposition. The vociferous polemics of their critics cast an overlay of misunderstanding about the essence of the movement that lasted many decades. Most Muslim interlocutors encountered by Western representatives or travellers in the region either knew little of the Wahhābi credo or had good reason to misrepresent it. Sharīf Ghālib, Ottoman ruler of the Hijaz (d. 1816, r. 1787/8–1813), and his allies, who sought to entangle the Ottomans in his struggle with the Sa'ūdis, were particularly energetic purveyors of anti-Wahhābi tropes.[17] The conduct

[13] Letter of 18 November 1818, from Cairo.

[14] Letter of Consul-General Lt. Col. Ernest Missett in Alexandria to Under-Secretary Edward Cooke, Foreign Office, of 12 January 1814 (FO 24/5) in Burdett 2013 i: 395–6. Missett was British consul-general 1802–08 and 1811–15. British officials in India had made a closer study of Wahhābism and had a better grasp of its tenets.

[15] Bonacina 2015, *passim*.

[16] Wahhābi beliefs are outlined in Crawford 2014: 47–106.

[17] Burckhardt 1831 ii: 100, 183.

of the Wahhābis contributed. Their use of *takfīr* (the designation of another Muslim as an unbeliever) and sometimes indiscriminate violence, especially that perpetrated by bedouin elements, against other Muslims helped to embed an impression of Wahhābism as a new religion – which for bedouin, previously lightly touched by Islam, it effectively was.[18]

It took Jean Louis Burckhardt, the famous Swiss traveller supported by the London-based African Association, to supply the first accurate picture of the Wahhābis' beliefs and practices for Western readers in his *Notes on the Bedouins and the Wahabys*, a seminal work not published until 1830.[19] Aged just thirty-two, he had died in Cairo of dysentery in October 1817, just over a year before Bowes Wright appeared there, and while the fate of early Wahhābism was still in the balance. Meanwhile, such public information as was available about the Wahhābis in London came from occasional fragmentary items in *The Times*, which sometimes relied on the French *Le Moniteur*. Bowes Wright reflected a common misunderstanding in telling his friend Joe that Imam 'Abd Allāh's grandfather had founded the movement.[20] In fact, Amir 'Abd al-'Azīz (d. 1803) had been the pupil, protégé, and close associate of the eponymous founder, Muḥammad ibn 'Abd al-Wahhāb (1703–92), who had formed an alliance with 'Abd al-Azīz's father, Muḥammad ibn Sa'ūd (d. 1765).

Had Bowes Wright had any inkling he might encounter a Wahhābi himself, he might have spent time in Paris hunting down the informative, if still historically inaccurate, works of two former Napoleonic officials Louis de Corancez and J.B.L. Rousseau.[21] De Forbin, another former Bonapartist, whose travelogue of 1817–18 offers a valuable French counterpoint to Bowes Wright's account, and whose French mission in those years was despatched to acquire classical antiquities for the royal museums in Paris (of which he became director-general in 1815–16), had an equally distorted understanding of the Wahhābis' history. For

[18] Ibid. ii: 101–2.

[19] For an analysis of Burckhardt's vital contribution, see Bonacina 2015: 159–83.

[20] Letter of 18 November 1818, from Cairo.

[21] De Corancez, *Histoire des Wahabis*, first published in 1810 (English translation in *The History of the Wahabis*, Reading: Garnet, 1995); Rousseau, *Mémoire sur les Trois Plus Fameuses Sectes du Musulmanisme*, published in Paris and Marseille in 1818.

him their chief was 'Abdoul Massaoud'; al-Dir'iyya, their capital, was the capital of Yemen.[22]

The Englishman also reflected the views of the Egyptians and Ottomans in describing the imam as a 'rebel'. Bowes Wright would have understood this to mean that the Sa'ūdis had previously been, at least nominally, subjects of the sultan. In reality, Najd had always lain outside Ottoman domains. The Ottomans had had no footprint there other than through occasional, short-lived incursions by their appointee in the Hijaz, the sharīf of Mecca. That the sultan's name was mentioned in Najdi Friday prayers before the Wahhābis banned the practice as an illegitimate 'innovation' did not mean Najdis previously accepted Ottoman suzerainty.[23] Such reference to the Ottoman Sunni champion was traditional and conventional, presumably introduced in earlier centuries by Najdi clerics trained in Ottoman provincial capitals. It conveyed no local political import. When the Wahhābis banned mention of the sultan in Friday prayers in Najd and then at the Grand Mosque in Mecca in 1803, the move was driven not by subversive or hostile intent but by theological objection to all mention of rulers, the Āl Sa'ūd included.

The Sa'ūdi state emerged in a geopolitical no-man's land. Ibn 'Abd al-Wahhāb, the activist and preacher who initiated the Wahhābi movement, admitted that he would not have been able to spread his message within Ottoman dominions.[24] He had once tried in Basra and been chased out. Yet lack of political or military footprint in Najd did not deter the Ottomans from claiming overlordship of Najd and denouncing the Sa'ūdis as disobedient rebels, guilty of renouncing loyalty to the sultan. This was how the Wahhābis were seen in Cairo, and it was on this basis that the Ottomans and the pasha set out to exact retribution on Imam 'Abd Allāh and his companions. Unsurprisingly, Bowes Wright adopted the same viewpoint.

It is ironic that Muḥammad 'Alī, who genuinely was a subject of the sultan, was himself later to rebel against his master and to carve an empire for himself out of Ottoman dominions. Unlike the Sa'ūdi imams, he

---

22 De Forbin 1819: 286–7. Later he describes it as the capital of the Hijaz (1819: 308). Al-Jabartī called Sa'ūd 'Mas'ūd' (fortunate). The Ottomans often called him 'Sa'ūd ghayr al-mas'ūd' (the unfortunate Sa'ūd).

23 Ibn Ghannām 1949 i: 112–13, 132.

24 Ibid. i: 151–2.

threatened the very survival of the Ottoman state by occupying Palestine and Syria until forced to retreat under European pressure in 1840. He had been suspect in Ottoman eyes from the moment he achieved prominence in Cairo, generating an uneasiness that, for a period, was counteracted by Ottoman gratitude for his recovery of the Holy Cities and conquest of al-Dir'iyya. When he wrested the Holy Cities back from the Wahhābis, restoring the hajj and traditional religious practices, he did so in the name of the Ottoman sultan. But he took control of the Hijaz, its commerce and the Red Sea trade and kept them in his own hands for two decades. In solving one apparently intractable problem, the Ottomans created another.

Wahhābi destiny denied

Over seven decades, the Āl Sa'ūd had transformed themselves from petty rulers of a string of small settlements in Central Arabia in the early 1740s into the dominant power in the Arabian Peninsula. Throughout, they had championed the aggressive religious ideology of Ibn 'Abd al-Wahhāb. It had always been an article of Wahhābi faith that the worldly success of the movement, reflected in its military triumphs, the relentless expansion of Sa'ūdi territory, and the growing prosperity of its capital al-Dir'iyya, was incontrovertible evidence of God's favour and the eternal truth of the radical Wahhābi creed.

Late in life, Shaykh 'Abd al-Raḥmān ibn Ḥasan Āl al-Shaykh, the prominent grandson of Ibn 'Abd al-Wahhāb, rehearsed for his students the Wahhābis' regular refrain that God was on their side:

> We mention some of the experiences of [the early Wahhābis] at the hands of their enemies and God's assistance and help to them, despite their small numbers and weakness and the strength and great numbers of their enemy. There was a lesson here and proof for them that they were in the right and their enemy were in the wrong.[25]

The shaykh drew parallels with the Prophet's career and insisted that the Wahhābis in these times constituted the one group within the Islamic

[25] 'Abd al-Raḥmān Āl al-Shaykh 2005: 77.

community (*umma*) that remained on the right path, as laid down in the Quran.[26] Yet he too had tasted the bitterness and confusion of defeat, losing his son Muḥammad at the siege of al-Dirʿiyya.[27] He had been transported to Cairo with members of the Āl Saʿūd and other Āl al-Shaykh after the fall of al-Dirʿiyya to spend years of exile studying at al-Azhar, before returning to Najd in 1825/6 to head a revived Wahhābi religious establishment.[28]

Aggressive and intolerant in their approach to other Muslims, the Wahhābis had threatened to disrupt religious belief and culture across the Islamic world and to upend the regional political order. In the name of the Ottoman sultan, the pasha snatched this destiny from them, to their bewilderment both at the time and for decades afterwards. If the Wahhābi approach to Islamic belief and practice was correct, how could God have deserted them and made their final leader face his end at the hands of an ungodly enemy 1,500 miles from home, stripped of everything except his faith? The imam's example of personal fortitude and courage could have inspired later generations of Wahhābis. Instead, the difficulty they had in addressing this awkward question reduced him to a historical embarrassment.

---

[26] Ibid.: 77, 101–2.

[27] Ibn Bishr 1982–83 i: 419.

[28] Ibid. ii: 41–42.

CHAPTER 2

The Sultan's Grievances against the Wahhābis

Genesis of conflict and Sharīf Ghālib of Mecca

The Sublime Porte had little reason to concern itself with the Wahhābis so long as they confined their campaign for dominance to remote Central Arabia. The subsequent Sa'ūdi conquest of al-Aḥsā' in eastern Arabia in the mid-1790s caused the Ottoman *wālī* of Baghdad concern, since it opened up Iraq as a Wahhābi target. But this move onto the Gulf was at the outer reaches of Ottoman vision and left the Sublime Porte untroubled. It had more urgent domestic and foreign preoccupations that touched on the regime's very survival. In the provinces, it had no spare capacity to address the growing power of locally-based elites at the expense of those forces responsible to the central government. In the major Arab governorates, mamlūks, nominally slaves, who belonged to competing military households, mostly ruled for the Ottomans. Their factionalism, and loosening grip on local notables, tribes and economic resources, risked these provinces slipping from Istanbul's grasp.

Sultan Maḥmūd had originally hoped to deal with the Wahhābis from either Baghdad or Damascus, but the *wālīs* in those two metropolises, wrestling with their own challenges, had neither the motivation nor the resources to take effective action. The Sa'ūdis repulsed two punitive Ottoman incursions from southern Iraq with insulting ease, and in 1810 Imam Sa'ūd staged a surprise raid right up to the surrounds of Damascus. Neither of the Iraq nor Syria governorates, with their meagre resources, tribal turbulence, and competing commitments, could serve as a launchpad for a military campaign against the Wahhābis, whether directed at ejecting them from the Hijaz only or at suppressing them entirely.

Normally of interest to the Sublime Porte only at the hajj season, the Hijaz and the Holy Cities were central to Sultan Maḥmūd's worries about the Wahhābis. Dual governance arrangements there, which were unlike those in any other Ottoman province, had traditionally bred relentless rivalry between the ruling Hashemite sharīf, based in Mecca, and successive *wālī*s of Jidda, appointed annually by the Sublime Porte. The sharīf had the advantage of greater local knowledge and durability, especially as few *wālī*s lasted more than a couple of years, many dying at post, thanks to the unhealthy conditions (which may account for the Ottomans trying to send Muḥammad 'Alī there in 1805). Usually, the *wālī* commanded just a few hundred Ottoman soldiers and small janissary garrisons, but his options expanded at hajj time. Then, armed Ottoman caravans arrived from Syria and Egypt in a major logistical exercise that amounted almost to an annual reconquest of the Hijaz. This was the moment of maximum danger for the ruling *sharīf*, as the sultan, acting through the hajj amirs, could always find another sharīf from his disputatious family to take his place.

When the Wahhābi movement pushed into the Hijaz in the 1790s and intensified pressure on Sharīf Ghālib by disrupting supply lines, suborning the tribes and frightening settled populations, he complained to Istanbul and requested assistance. At this stage, he sought Ottoman funds with which to buy tribes' loyalty. Fearful that the Ottomans would loosen his political and commercial grip on the Hijaz at best, or depose or kill him at worst, he did not want to see their forces deployed on his territory and using it as a permanent base against the Wahhābis. He was doubtless also concerned at the social and economic impact on the Hijaz of its transformation into a warzone. As his situation deteriorated, he urged the despatch of soldiers and military supplies. Vainly, he insisted that Ottoman action be launched directly against al-Dir'iyya from Iraq, although he knew better than anyone that the Holy Cities would always be the sultan's priority.

Ottoman custodianship of Mecca and al-Madīna was vital to the sultan's legitimacy as well as his revived claim to the caliphate. When the Sa'ūdis captured the cities in 1803–06, they prevented Ottoman pilgrimage caravans from entering, while allowing those whose religious practices were acceptable to them to fulfil their hajj obligations. The hajj, which successive sharīfs had prevented the Wahhābis from performing on the same basis as other Sunnis, became a vehicle and opportunity for the Wahhābis to spread their vision of Islam to distant corners of the Islamic world. That message itself represented a heavy blow to the sultan's prestige within the empire and beyond. Wahhābi actions in the Holy Cities underlined his impotence in the face of their repudiation of his leadership of Sunni Islam, as did their broadcast conviction that the religion practised in his lands could not rightly be viewed as Islam at all. The Sa'ūdis represented a powerful threat to Ottoman interests and standing.

This was a perilous time for the newly enthroned Sultan Maḥmūd II. The Napoleonic Wars were being waged by superior powers around the empire's borders. Egypt, where the Ottomans exercised formal sovereignty, had been invaded, first by the French in 1798, then, less dramatically and successfully, by the British in 1807. The Sublime Porte had been fearful in 1798 that Napoleon, who was trying to seduce the occupied Egyptians with honeyed proclamations about the synergy between the French Revolution and Islam, would occupy the Holy Cities. This fear of a Christian attack on them persisted for some years.[1] The Wahhābis, apparently oblivious to the regional perception that they were undermining a unified Islamic response to this Christian threat, menaced their Hijazi enemies from the landside, massacred the inhabitants of al-Ṭā'if in early 1803, and forced Sharīf Ghālib to submit. This practised dissembler kowtowed and pretended to adopt Wahhābism.

Many Muslims were shocked by what they saw as Wahhābi opportunism and disloyalty to the wider Islamic cause, as well as to the Ottomans. The Sa'ūdis and Wahhābis did not acknowledge this perception at the time, and perhaps never registered it. They reserved their enmity for errant co-religionists in their own area, not for more distant Christian powers. Regrettably, the contemporaneous Wahhābi chronicle, which might have offered insights into their awareness of the issue, peters out a year or two before the French invasion of Egypt – inexplicably, since the author survived until early 1811.[2]

---

[1] See e.g. letter of Muḥammad 'Alī to the Sublime Porte of 9 March 1808, Arabic translated text in 'Abd al-Raḥīm 1999: 367.

[2] Ibn Ghannām 1949 ii: 248. See Ibn Bishr 1982–83 i: 310–11.

Within his own capital, the sultan was beset by challenges and infighting that had proved too much for the reformist Salīm III (dethroned in 1807 and assassinated in 1808), and for his usurping successor Muṣṭafā IV (overthrown and murdered in 1808). With his religious credentials and regional credibility at stake and the Holy Cities occupied by the Sa'ūdis, Sultan Maḥmūd was at a loss how to tackle the distant Wahhābi challenge. He was to tell Muḥammad 'Alī that he had not slept nor rested since ascending the throne, because the Holy Cities were in the grip of 'Ibn Sa'ūd'.[3]

The taking of the Prophet's treasures

No event so crystallised Ottoman anguish at the loss of the Holy Cities as Imam Sa'ūd's seizure on behalf of the Wahhābi community of the treasures lodged at the Prophet's tomb in al-Madīna in 1807. This sparked outrage among the Ottomans and in many communities across the Islamic world. The Egyptians were particularly angry because of their close association with Ottoman rule in the Hijaz and management of the pilgrimage.[4] In their eyes, this was a *cause célèbre* to go with other actions by the Sa'ūdis in the Holy Cities. These included the levelling of much-loved tombs and shrines in a campaign to enforce Wahhābi norms, condemned by many Muslims as sacrilegious. The contemporary Egyptian hagiographer of Muḥammad 'Alī even claimed the Wahhābis left the environs of the Prophet's mosque covered in urine and excrement.[5] For most Muslims, the removal of the treasures confirmed the disrespect for the Prophet displayed by the Wahhābis, who, in their campaign against polytheism, accused their critics of elevating him to a God-like plane.

The original impact of the event within the Ottoman Empire was overshadowed by the shocking overthrow of Sultan Salīm III by janissaries on 28 June 1807. This heralded a year of infighting, instability and policy confusion in Istanbul. Leading Hijazis worked hard as a special interest group to keep the issue of Wahhābi conduct in the Holy Cities in front of the Sublime Porte. In 1809, a group of Hijazi notables fled the Holy

---

3 Mutawallī 1999: 90.

4 News of the stripping of the Prophet's tomb arrived in Cairo on 14 June 1807 (al-Jabartī 1958–67 vi: 381).

5 Al-Rajabī 1997: 127.

Cities and travelled to Istanbul to complain of the loss of their profitable hajj-related roles and made much of Wahhābi plundering of the Prophet's treasures.[6] When Imam Sa'ūd approached the pasha for a peace agreement in November 1813, Muḥammad 'Alī made the return of the treasures and compensation for those that had been disposed of one of the conditions for any peace treaty.[7] He again made their return one of a series of (harsh) terms for any permanent settlement with the Wahhābis in 1815.

To Sultan Maḥmūd, who acceded in 1808, and to the Sublime Porte, Imam Sa'ūd's seizure of the treasures was a calculated act of despoliation. It was yet another affront to members of the Ottoman dynasty, who had donated so many of the precious items over the centuries. It underlined the Sa'ūdis' blatant rejection of the Ottomans' religious and historical heritage in the Holy Cities Mecca and al-Madīna and humiliated them in the eyes of believers by underlining their failure to protect the Holy Cities. There were even insulting parallels with the Wahhābi pillage in April 1802 of Imam Ḥusayn's mausoleum in the Shī'i shrine city of Karbalā' in Iraq. The Ottoman rulers in Baghdad had conspicuously failed to defend this sacred site for the Shī'a. The Sa'ūdis and Sunni tribes overran and rampaged through the town with much bloodshed. Were the Prophet's treasures in al-Madīna to be treated as booty on a par with those seized from this Shī'i mausoleum?

In Karbalā', with a violence and rapacity that sent a collective shiver of fear through anti-Wahhābi towns across the Arabian Peninsula, the attackers had destroyed the cupola over the grave and despoiled the tomb, taking the covering decorated with emeralds, rubies and precious stones. They were unable to break off many of the riveted gold plates on the mausoleum,[8] but seized all the money, weapons, clothes, furnishings, gold, silver, valuable Qurans, and other items they found. Like the assembled treasures at the Prophet's tomb, this haul reflected an accumulation of donations from rulers and notables over centuries. Fatḥ 'Alī Shah (1772–1834) of Persia mobilised his forces and wrote sharply to Sulaymān Pasha of Baghdad, demanding revenge on the Wahhābis and issuing threats

---

[6] Al-Jabartī 1958–67 vii: 47.

[7] Ibid. vii: 227; Daḥlān 1887/88: 296–7.

[8] O'Quinn 2009: 325.

of intervention.[9] Thanks to the shah's strong and enduring interest, and the consequent awkwardness of the issue for the Ottoman sultan, 'Abd Allāh was to find himself being interrogated about the precious items from Karbalā', as well as the Prophet's treasures, in Istanbul.

Wahhābi justifications for stripping the Prophet's tomb

The Wahhābis objected to worship at tombs, viewing this as polytheism. Shrines created idols that encouraged illegitimate intercession between humans and God (even if, exceptionally, the Prophet was a valid intercessor). That rituals and practices at shrines involved a waste of resources by pilgrims or devotees was one of Ibn 'Abd al-Wahhāb's constant themes. Exploited by the self-proclaimed custodians of such tombs, visitors spent precious funds on fees and offerings that could be devoted to more useful religious and social purposes. In a characteristically hectoring tone, Imam Sa'ūd outlined Wahhābi doctrines to Sulaymān Pasha (d. 1819), *wālī* of Damascus 1810–12, in a letter of December 1810. He instructed him that proper Muslims were under a duty to destroy such shrines, once they had the power to do so.[10] The Wahhābi principle was that, when the tomb was located in a mosque, the mosque too was to be demolished if it had been built because of the tomb. If the tomb had been added later, the mosque could stand, but the tomb should be removed.[11] In any event, cupolas on tombs had to be destroyed, as these were signs of unbelief (*kufr*).[12]

Because of the Prophet's exceptional status, the Sa'ūdis, on taking al-Madīna, allowed his tomb to remain in a corner of the Prophet's mosque, even if they tried unsuccessfully to demolish the cupola above that corner. They forbade pilgrims from travelling to visit the tomb, as opposed to the mosque.[13] Offerings to the servants of the Prophet (i.e. those involved in looking after the tomb) were to be devoted to the interests of the 'Muslims',

---

[9] Qāyā 2008: 36.

[10] Letter of Imam Sa'ūd to Sulaymān Pasha of 11 December 1810 in Ibn Qāsim 1996–99 i: 287–316, at 299.

[11] *Responsum* of Shaykh 'Abd Allāh ibn Muḥammad ibn 'Abd al-Wahhāb in Ibn Qāsim 1996–99 iv: 265.

[12] *Responsum* of Shaykh 'Abd Allāh ibn Muḥammad ibn 'Abd al-Wahhāb in ibid. v: 88.

[13] Burckhardt 1831 ii: 200.

to be disbursed by the imam for the purposes of jihad, propagation or the welfare of the poor. If funds of this kind were located beyond Wahhābi territory, anyone could take them, for they were condemned and should not be left in place.[14]

The Sa'ūdis' appropriation of the treasures was consistent with their general ban on shrines and the rituals and practices associated with them. They were concerned that many of the precious items donated to the Prophet's tomb were in fact votive offerings, i.e. donors had been looking for a favour from God in return for the gift, in flagrant breach of the doctrine of God's oneness (*tawḥīd*). In late 1810, Imam Sa'ūd illustrated the point to Sulaymān Pasha in Damascus by citing a letter he had found in the Prophet's tomb in 1807. This was from Salīm III to the Prophet and had been delivered by a cousin. It requested the Prophet's help against the Christians and others. A contemptuous Sa'ūd saw this as conclusive evidence that the Ottomans lied about being true Muslims. In his view, the letter was outright unbelief (*kufr*). If that was the approach of the elite, what could one expect of the common people? He asserted that there were many other examples of similar letters in the Prophet's tomb contributed by both elite and general populace.[15]

For Sa'ūd to accuse a recently deposed sultan of committing *kufr* in person was characteristic of his fearless denunciation and defiance of the Ottomans in his heyday. His message, conveyed in an elaborately prepared epistle written on a large, impressive sheet under his seal, had the support, at least formally on paper, of Sharīf Ghālib, the *muftīs* of the four Sunni schools in Mecca, and *'ulamā'* in al-Madīna, all of whom added their seals as witnesses.[16] Ghālib's endorsement, with its description of Sa'ūd as *imām al-muslimīn*, public *mea culpa* about previous religious practices in the Holy Cities, and starkly aggressive Wahhābi tone must have been galling for him to sign. The Ottomans would have appreciated that he and the other Hijazi signatories were acting under duress, but their stamps added weight and authority, in wider Islamic terms, to Sa'ūd's views on shrines and the Prophet's tomb, as on other topics.

---

[14] *Responsum* of Shaykh 'Abd Allāh ibn Muḥammad ibn 'Abd al-Wahhāb in Ibn Q̧āsim 1996–99 ix: 317–8.

[15] Letter of Imam Sa'ūd to Sulaymān Pasha of 11 December 1810 in ibid. i: 304.

[16] A facsimile is in Dārat al-Malik 'Abd al-'Azīz 2000: 77.

Sa'ūd told Sulaymān Pasha that the funds devoted to shrines should be dedicated to serving the interests of Muslims. The Muslim leader (imam) was not merely permitted to disburse such funds on jihad and other such activities, he was under an obligation to do so.[17] Later, the Wahhābis justified the appropriation of the treasures from the Prophet's tomb on utilitarian grounds, applying this general principle to the special circumstances of the time. They noted that the Ottomans had ceased in 1807 to send the annual Ottoman subsidies (*ṣurra*) and gifts to the notables and people of al-Madīna, as well as of Mecca, that had previously accompanied the hajj cavalcade, which had as its centrepiece the ceremonial *maḥmal* (sacred litter mounted on a camel) from Egypt. The loss of these traditional subventions had placed the Holy Cities, both notables and the poor, under intense economic pressure.

With Istanbul overtaken by political turmoil and infighting, it was Muḥammad 'Alī who took it on himself to suspend the practice of the *ṣurra*, which conventionally was closely linked with the Egyptian hajj. He arranged for a *fatwā* from the *'ulamā'* to 'compel' him to suspend it on the grounds that the previous year the *ṣurra* had ended up in the wrong hands, its administrator (*amīn al-ṣurra*) hurt, and the *maḥmal* burnt.[18] Understandably, the Sublime Porte did not accede thereafter to Imam Sa'ūd's presumptuous request that it resume despatch of the subsidies because of the harm done to the Holy Cities by their suspension.[19] It is not clear why the Sa'ūdis supposed the Ottomans would be ready to help subsidise their occupation of the Holy Cities.

Sixty years later, Shaykh 'Abd al-Laṭīf ibn 'Abd al-Raḥmān Āl al-Shaykh, the head of the Wahhābi religious establishment who had spent his formative years in Cairene exile, declared that, with the withholding of the sultan's funds that year, harsh local conditions had left the Sa'ūdis with no option but to use the treasures to make up the funding shortfall at a time of economic hardship. They had relied on the authority granted at the time by the *muftīs* of the four law schools in al-Madīna, who issued *fatwās* (the texts of which we do not have). These apparently insisted,

[17] Letter of Imam Sa'ūd to Sulaymān Pasha of 11 December 1810 in Ibn Qāsim 1996–99 i: 300.

[18] Letter of Muḥammad 'Alī to the Sublime Porte of 1807 (no specific date given), Arabic translated text in 'Abd al-Raḥīm 1983: 40–1.

[19] Al-Sarhan 2016: 198.

unanimously, that it was the ruler's duty, not simply his right, to disburse the treasures from the Prophet's tomb to meet the urgent needs of the inhabitants of al-Madīna, especially the poor. The Prophet had no need of them, nor had he required such treasures to be hoarded. Indeed, he had forbidden just this kind of behaviour, demanding that, like wealth in the hands of kings and sultans, gold and silver should be expended for God's purposes, especially through distributions to the poor. What was the benefit in hoarding the treasures when the people of al-Madīna were in dire need?[20]

Contemporary Egyptian chronicler al-Jabartī records the Wahhābis' haul as including: four crates of jewels decorated with diamonds and precious stones of great value; four candlesticks with emeralds, with the candle replaced by an oblong diamond that shone in the dark; and about a hundred swords with their scabbards covered in pure gold and encrusted with diamonds and precious stones, their hilts decorated with emeralds, jade, etc., and their blades made of decorated iron, each sword of unassessable value and bearing the stamps of kings, bygone caliphs, and such like.[21] His views on these treasures chimed with those of the Wahhābis. In his opinion, the treasures had originally been lodged in the tomb as a reserve to be drawn on for jihad or to help defend against enemies. With the passage of time, they had come to be treated as the property of the Prophet that no one could take or disburse. This was against the Prophet's own personal example. He had never hoarded worldly goods in his lifetime and had "chosen to be a Prophet who was a slave [of God], not a Prophet who owned property".[22]

This passage raises squarely the question of ownership of the items in the Prophet's chamber (*ḥujra*). As al-Jabartī commented, many Muslims treated them as if they were the Prophet's own possessions, although ruling dynasties that had donated them saw them as heirlooms lodged at the tomb, in which they retained a special proprietary interest, and of which they remained the remote guardians. This was the attitude of the Ottomans, as exemplified by the phraseology of the famous Ottoman statesman and historian Aḥmed Cevdet Pasha (d. 1895), who, in his

---

[20] *Risāla* of ʿAbd al-Laṭīf ibn ʿAbd al-Raḥmān Āl al-Shaykh in Riḍā 1928 iii: 451–2.

[21] Al-Jabartī 1958–67 vii: 49.

[22] See ibid. vii: 47–8.

account of Imam 'Abd Allāh's interrogation, equates the Prophet's tomb with the royal store of valuables (*khazīna*).[23] This explains why in 1919, when the Ottomans lost control of al-Madīna for good, the treasures had already been restored to Istanbul, together with books and manuscripts from the libraries donated by the Ottomans. This was arranged in good time by Fakhrī Pasha, the stalwart final Ottoman governor, who insisted on his duty to protect the Prophet's tomb until finally forced to surrender. By contrast, the Wahhābis viewed the treasures as belonging to the Islamic community. This meant that, in their eyes, the treasures could, and should, be deployed in that community's interests at times of emergency. Since they, the Wahhābis, constituted that community, it was for their imam as its leader to decide whether and how the treasures were to be used during a period of economic distress.

This was the basis on which Imam Sa'ūd, with al-Jabartī's endorsement, took the Prophet's treasures. But, in an unusual digression in his chronicle that reveals his own attitudes and disapproval of Muḥammad 'Alī's practices and policies, the historian uses his discussion of the issue to express a forceful political viewpoint:

> Were the one hoarding [the treasure in the Prophet's tomb] to ask: "Is this treasure for the vicissitudes of the age to help with jihad against the unbelievers (*kuffār*) and polytheists, in case of need?", we would say: "We have seen the terrible need of the kings of our time and the way they have been forced to conciliate those who have triumphed over them. They have established close connections with the Afranj [Europeans] and emptied their treasuries of funds, exhausting them through bad organization, vainglory, and luxurious living.... They have set out to make money from their subjects by increasing their taxes, confiscations, and demands, and by seizing property without right, so that they beggar their merchants and subjects. Yet they still don't take any of the hoarded items.... If an item ends up in that place [the tomb], no one benefits from it, unless it is pilfered by the eunuchs known as the *āghās* of the Ḥaram. The poor among the Prophet's followers, the *'ulamā'*, the needy and travellers die of hunger, while

23 1874 xi: 60.

these treasures are forbidden items to which they are not allowed to gain access."[24]

This biting criticism of contemporary Islamic rulers and submission to European powers is all the more pointed because the chronicler goes straight on to note the pasha's infliction of yet more taxes on the people.[25] Yet, in his digression on the Prophet's treasures, al-Jabartī does not pinpoint the risk that, once rulers drew on them as a financial reserve, they might be misappropriated. Nor does he highlight the potential flaw in Wahhābi justifications for Imam Sa'ūd's actions. As he knew, the available evidence contradicted the suggestion that the Sa'ūdis disbursed the proceeds purely for the benefit of the local inhabitants or the poor, or exclusively in the interests of the Islamic community. Instead, many notables seem to have benefited personally, including members of the Āl Sa'ūd, and none more than the opportunistic and acquisitive Sharīf Ghālib.

Muḥammad 'Alī exploits the Wahhābi threat

Muḥammad 'Alī aimed to extract as much propaganda benefit as he could from casting the Sa'ūdi removal of the treasures as sacrilege and himself in the part of avenger on behalf of the wider Islamic community. This approach had particular appeal for him at a time when traditionalists, like chronicler al-Jabartī, were muttering against him for his ruthless programme to reform government and the economy, and for his closeness to the Europeans ('Afranj'). The ploy also fitted with a broader pattern of the pasha turning the Wahhābi threat to his personal advantage. Inadvertently, the Sa'ūdis were to play a crucial role at various points in his advancement.

There had been extended disorder in Cairo for years after the French occupation of 1798–1801, and notables and merchants were eager for security. For many in the capital, Muḥammad 'Alī represented the best prospect for political stability and for keeping at bay not only French and English invaders, but also the Wahhābis. The latter were making incursions into the Ottoman provinces of Syria and Iraq, as well as disrupting Egypt's vital trade with the Hijaz. The pasha's justification

[24] 1958–67 vii: 49.

[25] Ibid. vii: 50.

for not immediately transferring his forces to the Hijaz for an anti-Wahhābi campaign was that he feared stripping Egypt of its defences against potential European aggression – a genuine concern.[26] But he also employed delaying tactics to consolidate his position vis-à-vis successive Ottoman sultans and make them dependent on him. He used the interval to centralise power domestically and build up the materiel and resources to reinforce his own domination of local politics.

Before being compelled to confirm Muḥammad ʿAlī as *wālī*, the Sublime Porte, nervous at the strength of his local standing and viewing him as something of a rebel,[27] tried in vain to transfer him out of Egypt. Thereafter it harboured doubts about his intentions,[28] while he blamed others for spreading false rumours about him.[29] Patiently and single-mindedly, he outmanoeuvred the Sublime Port, deftly using Ottoman authorities' increasingly strident calls for action against the Wahhābis - and their reliance on him to recover the Holy Cities - to both entrench his own power and gain greater autonomy for the province. The menace of the Wahhābis gave him the leverage with his suzerain to ensure that he remained undisturbed in office. Not for the first time, Saʿūdi expansionism spurred political changes in an Ottoman provincial capital, changes that worked ultimately to al-Dirʿiyya's disadvantage. In Cairo, the Wahhābis served unwittingly as the catalyst for their most dangerous enemy's consolidation of political, military and economic power

By 1810, Muḥammad ʿAlī was ready to display both defiance of Istanbul and ruthless independence of action. In that year, Sultan Maḥmūd sacked the *wālī* of Damascus, Yūsuf Kunj, whose pen-friendship with the pasha was grounded in anti-Saʿūdi campaign planning. To Muḥammad ʿAlī's alarm, the sultan replaced him with Sulaymān Pasha, a former mamlūk of Aḥmad Pasha al-Jazzār of Acre, with links to the Egyptian mamlūks. Muḥammad ʿAlī soon came to believe that this man, who, as we have

---

[26] Letters of Muḥammad ʿAlī to the Sublime Porte of mid- to late February 1808 and 9 March 1808, Arabic translated texts in ʿAbd al-Raḥīm 1999: 363–4, 366.

[27] Letter of Missett to Cooke of 7 July 1813 (FO 24/4), text in Burdett 2013 i: 340–4, at 341.

[28] See e.g. letter of Muḥammad Najīb to Muḥammad ʿAlī of 20 December 1810, Arabic translated text in ʿAbd al-Raḥīm 1983: 138–43.

[29] Letter to the sultan of 9 August 1811, Arabic translated text in ʿAbd al-Raḥīm 1983: 177–82, at 180.

seen, was soon under intense Sa'ūdi pressure, was plotting against him.[30] The disgraced Yūsuf, under threat of execution, fled and sought refuge in Egypt with Muḥammad 'Alī, who received him with some fanfare.[31] The pasha, who had an enduring interest in controlling Syria and its resources, demanded that the Ottomans pardon and reinstate Yūsuf, arguing that this would serve the interests of the Hijaz campaign, since Sulaymān Pasha was conspiring against him.[32] This push to have Yūsuf reappointed to Damascus failed, although the sultan did pardon him.[33]

Muḥammad 'Alī still did not let the matter drop. In late February 1811, he placed his younger son, Ṭūsūn Pasha (1793–1816), in command of the troops going to the Hijaz, and ordered the forces to encamp at Qubbat al-'Izab in Cairo. He also suggested he was preparing a military expedition under a senior mamlūk commander to restore Yūsuf. He asked the astrologers to pick a time to invest his son with the 'cloak of travel'. They chose Friday 2 March at 4 p.m. and the pasha had criers summon mamlūk notables to the citadel next day in their finest attire.

On arrival in the citadel, the mamlūk amirs sat with the pasha and drank coffee. There was then a parade. Muḥammad 'Alī had the gates closed and the mamlūks (or "Beys", as Bowes Wright calls them) were trapped. Their massacre by the pasha's Albanian troops ensued,[34] with the pasha sitting cross-legged with his pipe watching from the battlements, according to de Forbin's description.[35] Mamlūk remnants, not caught in the slaughter or subsequent Albanian sweep through Cairo, regrouped in Upper Egypt. They were reported by the British consul to be in touch with the Wahhābis (and French), indeed to have become Wahhābis and allied with the Sa'ūdis. Muḥammad 'Alī too expressed concern to Istanbul

---

[30] Letter of Muḥammad 'Alī to the Sublime Porte of 25 September 1810, Arabic translated text in 'Abd al-Raḥīm 1999: 402–4, at 402.

[31] Al-Jabartī 1958–67 vii: 117–18.

[32] Note from Sulaymān Thābit to the grand vizier of 19 September 1810, Arabic translated text in 'Abd al-Raḥīm 1983: 123–5; letter of Muḥammad 'Alī to Muḥammad Najīb of 1 January 1811, Arabic translated text in 'Abd al-Raḥīm 1999: 408–10.

[33] Letter of Muḥammad 'Alī to the Sublime Porte of 25 March 1811, Arabic translated text in 'Abd al-Raḥīm 1983: 163–5.

[34] Al-Jabartī 1958–67 vii: 127–32.

[35] 1819: 229–31.

about some of the mamlūks joining forces with the Wahhābis.[36] British Consul-General Missett (d.1820), whose strong powers of observation were not matched by soundness of judgment, commented in alarmist terms:

> Should the Wahabees, under the guidance of the Mamlooks, make an irruption into this country, there is every reason to fear that they would meet with little resistance.... The Egyptians in general are so cruelly oppressed, that any change must appear advantageous to them. Nor is it probable that the Viceroy would be cordially supported by his troops.[37]

It remains unclear what evidence there was for this improbable alliance between Wahhābis and mamlūks, for they had little in common but shared hostility to the pasha. Furthermore, the mamlūks had been driven down into southern Egypt, whereas any Saʿūdi incursion would have had to come through Sinai.

With the mamlūk challenge largely eliminated, Muḥammad ʿAlī used military and logistical preparations for his anti-Wahhābi military campaign to build up his forces, exert a greater grip on the economy, and concentrate power in his own hands. Later, there were suggestions from foreign observers that the pasha was exploiting the war to tie up, and reduce the numbers and strength of, his unruly Albanian forces. He appeared to Bernardino Drovetti (1776–1852), French consul 1805–15 and 1821–29, who was close to Muḥammad ʿAlī, to be indifferent to their losses, and slow to send reinforcements.[38] Albanian elements were still a dangerous source of instability in 1815. When the traveller and later MP William Bankes (1786–1855) arrived in Cairo, they were rioting and pillaging the bazaars, while the pasha, unsure of the loyalty of the troops he had with him, remained locked up in the citadel.[39] The rebellious Albanians remained a formidable obstacle to the pasha's ambitions to establish a new model army of Egyptian soldiers.

---

[36] Letter of Muḥammad ʿAlī to the Sublime Porte of 3 November 1810, Arabic translated text in ʿAbd al-Raḥīm 1999: 405–7, at 406.

[37] Letter of Missett to Foreign Secretary Marquis of Wellesley of 25 March 1812 (FO 24/4), text in Burdett 2013 i: 317–20, at 318–9, quotation at 319–20 (see also his enclosed letter to his representative in Cairo, ibid. i: 321).

[38] Ridley n.d.: 57–8.

[39] De Forbin 1819: 287; Usick 2002: 24, 26. See below p. 38.

The pasha makes a dangerous last resort for the sultan

Sultan Maḥmūd and his predecessors had tried in vain to mobilise the governors of Baghdad and Damascus to crush the Wahhābis. It was in desperation, and probably not without apprehension, that Maḥmūd resorted to the astute Muḥammad 'Alī in Cairo as his instrument to restore the old order in Arabia, especially in the Holy Cities. The pasha, preoccupied initially with domestic threats and fearing external attack from any of the French, English or even Ottomans, kept the sultan impatiently on edge, as the Sublime Porte's other military options evaporated.

The expedient of turning to Muḥammad 'Alī carried longer-term costs for Maḥmūd that plagued him until the end of his reign. The wily, ruthless pasha was no one's catspaw and was already establishing his independence of the Sublime Porte in Cairo. He had no intention of re-instituting the old order and many years would pass before Ottoman control returned to the Hijaz in anything but name. The pasha was ultimately able to pursue a campaign against al-Dir'iyya that played to his own strategic ambitions more than it matched the sultan's narrower geopolitical gameplan. The success of this in 1816–18 gave him a launchpad for regional expansion and taste for foreign adventurism that, until the final dénouement in 1840, would take his forces to the Gulf and then into Morea (the Peloponnese), Palestine and Syria.

In late 1818, all this lay ahead. At this point, with his forces having occupied the Hijaz, invaded Najd and razed al-Dir'iyya, it still suited him to play the part of the sultan's loyal instrument. He would underline the service he had done his suzerain, and the debt the sultan owed him, by despatching to the imperial capital the captive Sa'ūdi imam in response to his master's instructions. Accompanying him were the remaining Prophet's treasures taken by the imam's father.

Many years later, in 1840, when the pasha's foreign adventurism at the expense of the Ottomans had fallen foul of the European powers and Maḥmūd II was dead, Muḥammad 'Alī insisted in a letter to the French that his Hijaz campaigning had not been driven by his own ambitions. On the contrary, he had been enticed by favours offered by the sultan and keen to be viewed as among the Ottoman state's defenders. His recapture of the Holy Cities had been a service to the Islamic faith and the Ottoman Empire, and his wars in the Hijaz had had absolutely no other goal than to serve his nation and his sovereign.[40] This was indeed the kind of language he used with the Sublime Porte at the time. Yet, on reading this letter, British ministers and officials, who had just wrested Ottoman Syria and Palestine from oppressive occupation by Ibrāhīm Pasha's forces, would surely have allowed themselves wry smiles at the elderly ruler's unconvincingly pious explanation of his own motives.

---

[40] Undated, translated letter of Muḥammad 'Alī to M. Cochelet in French, attached to letter of Consul-General in Alexandria (Colonel) G. Lloyd Hodges to Foreign Secretary Viscount Palmerston of 21 January 1840 (FO 78/404), text in Burdett 2013 i: 721–7 at 722, 725. The French government had instructed Cochelet to ask what the pasha's intentions were towards the Hijaz.

CHAPTER 3

The Pasha Invades the Hijaz, Purges it of Enemies, and Treats Peace as a Trap

The first Arabian campaign

The war between the Ottoman-Egyptian expeditionary forces and the Wahhābis began in August 1811. It was then that the pasha finally acceded to what had started as peremptory commands and ended as desperate entreaties from the Sublime Porte to subdue the Wahhābis. He had endured many months of constant chivvying from Istanbul, even as he embarked on elaborate preparations for expeditionary warfare in harsh terrain, where he knew local allies would be fickle. His invasion of the Hijaz, involving the despatch of cavalry and camels by land and troops by sea, that saw the seizure of the bridgehead of Yanbuʿ in October, was a remarkable logistical achievement. Thereafter, the campaign under the command of his second oldest son, the engaging but young and inexperienced Ṭūsūn, had mixed success.

The war was brutal from the outset. When the expeditionary force first took Yanbuʿ, the soldiery plundered everything there, including goods, money, cloths, coffee etc., and then abused the women and girls, taking them prisoner and selling them amongst one another.[1] In a strong tone of disapproval, al-Jabartī recounted a senior officer explaining an early defeat to him as grounded in the origins, culture and conduct of the soldiery. Most soldiers belonged to another religious community (*milla*). Some had no religion and did not belong to any school of law (*madhhab*).

---

[1] Al-Jabartī 1958–67 vii: 144.

There were no prayer calls in camp, and observance of Islamic rituals and practices, such as prayer, did not so much as occur to the soldiery. Instead, they drank alcohol, committed fornication and sodomy, levied interest, and fought each other. On seizing the town of Badr to the south-east of Yanbuʿ, they took the wives, daughters and sons even of *ʿulamāʾ* and sold them to each other, saying they were unbelievers (*kuffār*) and "Khawārij", referring to the group in early Islam judged to have rebelled against the community (this was a derogatory term for the Wahhābis much used by the Ottomans and other enemies). When one upright inhabitant of the town asked a soldier to return his wife, the soldier told him she would spend the night with him and he would return her in the morning.[2] Such unbridled conduct, which contrasted with the traditions of warfare practised by the settled elements of Najd and bedouin, set the tone for the conflict.

The expeditionary force suffered an early defeat at the hands of the future Imam ʿAbd Allāh, in the mountainous area of Wadi al-Ṣafrāʾ at a mid-point between Yanbuʿ and al-Madīna in December 1811. The troops, caught unawares by the enemy and outumbered, fled, leaving their artillery, equipment and supplies. More than 4,000 Ottomans died, as against around 600 of the Wahhābis, according to the Saʿūdi chronicler.[3] This put paid to initial over-confidence on the part of the Ottoman commanders. Muḥammad ʿAlī duly sent reinforcements and Ṭūsūn devoted more effort and resources to gaining the support of local tribal chiefs through bribery and pressure. This brought results. Al-Madīna fell to the invaders in 1812. In the following year, ʿAbd Allāh yielded Mecca without a fight, al-Ṭāʾif likewise fell, and Sharīf Ghālib declared for the Ottomans. The latter still suffered costly military setbacks, including at Turaba in mid-1813 and at al-Qunfudha. The main urban centres of the Hijaz were in their hands, but Saʿūdi raids kept the expeditionary force under pressure. With the Sublime Porte's encouragement, Muḥammad ʿAlī resolved to examine the situation for himself. In late 1813, he appeared in Jidda with further reinforcements.

---

2 Ibid. vii: 151–2.

3 Ibn Bishr 1982–83 i: 322–6. The young *qāḍī* ʿAbd al-Raḥmān Āl al-Shaykh was an eye-witness to this victory, which he describes in 2005: 111–14.

A well-trodden route to execution or exile

In establishing his grip on the Hijaz, the pasha was determined to eliminate not only leading Wahhābis, especially those from the area and with strong local followings or influence. He also aimed to remove Hijazis who might represent independent or alternative poles of power. Because of the Ottomans' formal status in the Holy Cities, he could not expect to establish the same kind of monopoly of political and economic power that he was working to achieve in Egypt, but he could install suitable puppets to guarantee him control. Imam 'Abd Allāh was to be neither the first exiled Arabian leader despatched to Cairo by the pasha, nor the first prominent Wahhābi to travel on to execution in Istanbul.

'Uthmān al-Muḍāīfī, a turncoat who was Sharīf Ghālib's brother-in-law and minister before giving allegiance to Imam Sa'ūd and becoming an effective Sa'ūdi commander, including at Wadi al-Ṣafrā', was captured by the sharīf east of his home town of al-Ṭā'if in September 1813 and put in irons.[4] Handed over to Muḥammad 'Alī's forces, he was escorted to Cairo, via Jidda, in early November 1813. In Jidda he narrowly missed the arrival of the pasha. Once in Cairo, where the citadel's cannons fired in celebration, he entered the city on a camel so that everyone could see him. A procession took him to the citadel where he was greeted by senior officials.[5] After three days, he proceeded on to Istanbul accompanied by Muḥammad Najīb Effendi Qubbī, the pasha's longstanding representative there. On arrival at the imperial capital, the pasha's youngest son, Ismā'īl (1795–1822), presented him ceremoniously, with the keys to the recaptured Ka'ba, to the sultan.[6]

Al-Muḍāīfī made a positive impression during his transit in Cairo. After a congenial evening with him at the citadel, the senior Egyptians in the pasha's absence lamented that a fine, well-spoken man of such authority was destined for Istanbul and execution.[7] That individual Wahhābis could be civilised, well-educated and eloquent always seemed to astonish their interlocutors in the great metropolises of the Middle East. It contradicted the popular view in these urban centres that the Wahhābis were uncouth

---

4 Ibn Bishr 1982–83 i: 334–6; Daḥlān 1887/88: 296.

5 Al-Jabartī 1958–67 vii: 226–7.

6 Burckhardt 1831 ii: 248.

7 Al-Jabartī 1958–67 vii: 227; Daḥlān 1887/88: 296.

bedouin savages from the barren wastes of Arabia, meriting as much disdain as dread.

Mas'ūd ibn Muḍayyān, Sa'ūdi amir of al-Madīna, was another prominent Wahhābi captive executed in Istanbul. He had been taken prisoner in 1813 after surrendering under a safe conduct, which his enemy breached.[8] He had become governor of al-Madīna and head of the powerful Ḥarb tribe on the death of his brother from smallpox in 1806, some years after they had sworn allegiance to the Sa'ūdis.[9] 1806 was the year the Āl Muḍayyān played a key role in the final subjugation of al-Madīna. Once it was in their hands, the Sa'ūdis destroyed the cupolas over graves and shrines on Imam Sa'ūd's orders, even if the solidity of the dome over the Prophet's mosque defied their efforts.[10] Ibn Muḍayyān, a committed Wahhābi, was governor when Imam Sa'ūd stripped the Prophet's tomb in the following year. He and the Ḥarb were then largely responsible for the Sa'ūdi victory at Wadi al-Ṣafrā' in December 1811.[11] Thereafter, he led sizeable forces against Muḥammad 'Alī's troops, with some success,[12] and was viewed by the pasha as a close friend of Imam Sa'ūd.[13] This explains why the pasha deemed him worth despatching to the Ottoman capital.

A letter Muḥammad 'Alī wrote to his Istanbul representative on 18 March 1813 points to Ibn Muḍayyān accompanying Ismā'īl to Istanbul.[14] By contrast, al-Jabartī suggests he preceded al-Muḍāīfī there in the company of Laṭīf Āghā, who was sent in advance of Ismā'īl Pasha with news of the recovery of the Holy Cities and received with much fanfare and celebration. He says that, after execution on the day of his arrival,

[8] Burckhardt 1831 ii: 241–2. Burckhardt claims that al-Muḍāīfī and Ibn Muḍayyān were both betrayed by their 'Utaybi and Ḥarb bedouin hosts contrary to bedouin custom. Ibn Muḍayyān had just escaped from Ottoman forces (ibid. ii: 242, 248). See also al-Ḥarbī 1996 i: 154–8.

[9] Burckhardt 1831 ii: 198–9; Ibn Bishr 1982–83 i: 288; al-Ḥarbī 1996 i: 141, 145–6.

[10] Burckhardt 1831 ii: 109–10; Ibn Bishr 1982–83 i: 288.

[11] Ibn Bishr 1982–83 i: 324–5.

[12] Al-Bassām 2010: 54–7.

[13] Letter of Muḥammad 'Alī to the Sublime Porte of 21 November 1811, Arabic translated text in 'Abd al-Raḥīm 1983: 202.

[14] Letter of Muḥammad 'Alī to Muḥammad Najīb of 18 March 1813, Arabic translated text in Mawjānī 2014: 379–80, at 379.

Ibn Muḍayyān's corpse was hung from the gate to the palace.[15] Whether Ibn Muḍayyān and al-Muḍāīfī reached Istanbul together or separately, they shared the same fate of being paraded through the streets of the Ottoman capital as popular spectacles before beheading.[16] Whether they were interrogated (and tortured) beforehand is unclear, but, in the midst of a continuing conflict that engaged the sultan so closely, the Ottomans would surely have questioned them under pressure. It was in vain that Imam Sa'ūd had offered the pasha in Jidda 100,000 riyals to secure al-Muḍāīfī's release and made overtures for a peace agreement. The pasha told Sa'ūdi emissaries bluntly that al-Muḍāīfī was already on his way to the sultan.[17]

Reports differ on whether Sa'ūd's amir in 'Asīr and the Tihāma, Ṭāmī ibn Shu'ayb, who had led the Wahhābis to victory at al-Qunfudha in early 1814 against a recently disembarked expeditionary force, perished in Cairo or Istanbul. According to the Sa'ūdi chronicler, he was sent to Cairo on his capture by the pasha's forces after the battle of Bisl in 1815 and crucified there, a spectacle doubtless designed to help convince the long-suffering local populace of military progress in western Arabia.[18] Ottoman records, by contrast, suggest that, after being taken to Cairo with the pasha and shown off there, he was sent on to Istanbul where he was paraded and executed.[19] Burckhardt supports this version and says that, on his capture, Ṭāmī had been taken to al-Qunfudha, where he was lodged near Muḥammad 'Alī, who "often conversed with him for amusement, as the tiger plays with his prey before he seizes it in his grasp". Ṭāmī's dignity and charisma impressed his captors, to the extent that the pasha promised to intercede with the Sublime Porte to have his sentence commuted to exile. Yet, on arrival in Cairo, Ṭāmī was displayed on a camel with the severed head of a fellow Wahhābi leader, whom the pasha had had cut to pieces by his bodyguards, in a bag suspended from his shoulders. The head went with him to Istanbul.[20]

---

[15] Al-Jabartī 1958–67 vii: 217, 228.

[16] Daḥlān 1887/88: 296.

[17] Al-Jabartī 1958–67 vii: 227; Daḥlān 1887/88: 296.

[18] Ibn Bishr 1982–83 i: 374–5.

[19] Ṣābān 2004: 91.

[20] Burckhardt 1831 ii: 332–4 (quotation at 333).

We do not know how far 'Abd Allāh was aware of the unsavoury ends of these Wahhābis, but gruesome tales may have filtered back to prey on his mind during his own final journey. He came from a tradition that handled captive adversaries differently. Wahhābis had a well-deserved reputation for treating their enemies harshly.[21] A prominent opponent, if seized on the field of battle, could expect to be killed. Away from the heat of conflict, the Wahhābis could be strikingly measured and flexible in handling influential or potential enemies who fell under their control. With the odd exception, they preferred to hold them close in al-Dir'iyya, rather than execute them ceremonially or even privately. They applied this approach early to numerous religious critics in Najd, including Ibn 'Abd al-Wahhāb's own brother, Sulaymān (d. 1794). They also made a practice of trying to convert emissaries arriving in al-Dir'iyya to Wahhābism (al-Muḍāīfī was a prominent example), and of lavishing hospitality and gifts on former enemies and Ottoman notables before escorting them safely home. Prominent figures hostile to their interests, whom they detained in al-Dir'iyya, included Hijazis such as Sharīf 'Abd Allāh ibn Surūr, and numerous Gulf shaykhs, among them members of the ruling Āl Khalīfa from Bahrain and the shaykh of the Qawāsim from Rās al-Khayma. Some of these negotiated their eventual release, others escaped. Unlike the Ottomans, the Sa'ūdis never saw the need to stage high-profile executions to encourage their own people.

Local notables pay the price for purloining the Prophet's treasures

Another prisoner, despatched to Istanbul and executed at the same time as Ibn Muḍayyān, according to Burckhardt, was the intriguing and unprepossessing figure of Ḥasan al-Qala'ī.[22] His very career illustrated the weak Ottoman grip on al-Madīna before the Sa'ūdis arrived. He was appointed commander of the al-Madīna citadel in the late 18th century. Of low birth, small of stature and almost lame, he was a violent thug with a gang of bedouin, North Africans and local lowlife at his disposal. He made himself undisputed master of the town, preying on and oppressing

[21] For example, Ibn 'Abd al-Wahhāb personally ordered the killing in 1753/4 of Sulaymān ibn Khuwayṭir, a close associate of his brother Sulaymān, who was a leading opponent (Ibn Bishr 1982–83 i: 68).

[22] 1831 ii: 242. Burckhardt calls him 'Hassan el Kaladjy'.

local residents and pilgrims, and seizing their property and the annual allowances sent from Istanbul. By these methods, he amassed considerable wealth, yet the Sublime Porte did nothing to address complaints about his organised criminality. When the Sa'ūdis started to advance against the town, he only intensified his violence and looting, and then led the resistance to the Sa'ūdi siege. He finally submitted to Imam Sa'ūd with the town's notables and *qāḍīs*, including the shaykh al-Ḥaram, in 1805–06, on condition that the imam let him remain in post as amir of the citadel.[23]

Still dominant in the town despite a Sa'ūdi garrison, Ḥasan al-Qala'ī adopted, or pretended to adopt, Wahhābism, but in 1812 Sa'ūd dismissed him and replaced him at the citadel with the trusty Ibrāhīm ibn 'Ufayṣān (d. 1814).[24] When Muḥammad 'Alī's forces besieged the citadel in 1812, al-Qala'ī put out feelers for a negotiated surrender, but Ṭūsūn's forces captured him, put him in irons, and subjected him to all kinds of torture before sending him to Egypt and then on to Istanbul.[25] As the pasha told his representative Muḥammad Najīb in Istanbul, he well merited execution.[26]

According to Burckhardt, before the Sa'ūdis had even occupied the town, Ḥasan al-Qala'ī had staged his own raid on the Prophet's treasures and distributed them among his followers.[27] Especially since he held an official post at the Prophet's tomb,[28] this would have been justification enough for sending him to the Sublime Porte for execution. On the other hand, Félix Mengin, the trader and former French consular agent in Cairo (1804–07), who in 1823 published an uncritical history of Egypt under Muḥammad 'Alī, and is generally a less reliable source than Burckhardt, reports that, when Imam Sa'ūd was leaving the tomb, he gave the keys to al-Qala'ī, who then lifted the remaining valuables for himself.[29] This prompted the flight to Syria of Shaykh al-Ḥaram 'Anbar Āghā, who was

---

[23] 'Abd al-Ghānī 1996: 396–7, 400–01. See Ibn Bishr 1982–83 i: 362.

[24] Ṣābān 2004: 4, 37.

[25] Ibn Bishr 1982–83 i: 329; 'Abd al-Ghānī 1996: 397.

[26] Letter of Muḥammad 'Alī to Muḥammad Najīb of 18 March 1813, Arabic translated text in Mawjānī 2014: 379–80, at 380.

[27] Burckhardt 1831 ii: 198.

[28] Al-Bassām 2010: 57.

[29] Mengin 1823 ii: 536.

dismissed by Sa'ūd in March 1807.[30] 'Anbar Āghā feared being accused of the deed – with good reason, since al-Qala'ī duly wrote to Sa'ūd blaming him.[31]

That al-Qala'ī with some of his followers participated in the raid on the tomb or took advantage of it to lay their hands on considerable loot for themselves is corroborated by a letter Ṭūsūn sent to his father in July 1813. Commenting that al-Qala'ī had shown great pleasure in serving Sa'ūd, Ṭūsūn said he had ensured that al-Qala'ī did not escape. He had tracked down some items from the tomb, and returned them there. Al-Qala'ī's torture was doubtless accompanied by close interrogation over his actions and the location of the treasures he and his acolytes had taken. Ṭūsūn suggested that al-Qala'ī would (and should) endure further questioning in Cairo and Istanbul.[32] As for 'Anbar, he had already been the subject of a report to the sultan in 1805/6 (i.e. before the Sa'ūdi takeover of al-Madīna), accusing him of filching pieces from the Prophet's tomb, as well as taking money from the 'purse' (*ṣurra*) donated annually by the sultan.[33] Burckhardt notes that, when Imam Sa'ūd came to the Prophet's tomb, the 'gold vessels' had already been removed.[34] Imam 'Abd Allāh was to tell the pasha that *āghā*s of the Ḥaram were among those who acquired treasures after the Sa'ūdis cleared the tomb.[35]

Whatever the timings of Ḥasan al-Qala'ī's and 'Anbar Āghā's removal of treasures from the tomb, it is clear that, during this disturbed period in the economically depressed (and dependent) Holy Cities, both Ottoman officials and local notables were prepared to help themselves to the treasures and the *ṣurra* for personal gain and to maintain themselves and their supporters in hard times. Imam Sa'ūd's expedient of resorting to the contents of the Prophet's tomb was far from the unheard-of, unprecedented act of desecration portrayed by the Ottomans and the pasha.

---

[30] Ibn Bishr 1982–83 i: 292.

[31] Mengin 1823 ii: 536.

[32] Letter of Ṭūsūn to Muḥammad 'Alī of 11 July 1813, Arabic translated text in Mawjānī 2014: 382–5, at 383–5.

[33] Zaydān 1975: 167–81. 'Anbar is reported as selling some of the items to Shaykh 'Abd al-Qādir Ilyās Effendi (only) and keeping the rest for himself (ibid.: 169).

[34] Burckhardt 1831 ii: 199.

[35] Al-Jabartī 1958–67 vii: 447.

The pasha exiles Sharīf Ghālib

Sharīf Ghālib, the Wahhābis' enduring adversary, was himself shortly to experience detention and transportation at the hands of Muḥammad 'Alī's troops, after they retook Mecca in 1813. Ghālib's longstanding fears for his own position were realised. Once the Ottoman military campaign had switched from Baghdad to Damascus and then Cairo, his predicament became acute, for he knew Muḥammad 'Alī distrusted him. He tried to play both sides, keeping in with the Sa'ūdis, while passing information and advice to the pasha.[36] Having expressed concern about the flexible loyalties of this slippery ruler for years, the pasha deposed him swiftly, and treacherously, in late 1813. The pasha appeared in Mecca with the Egyptian hajj caravan and a considerable body of troops, and duped Ghālib into calling on his son, Ṭūsūn Pasha. The pashas then seized him and his immediate family, occupied his palace, and set about seizing all the acquisitive sharīf's wealth and assets.[37] Such rough treatment of the still influential local ruler led many of the *ashrāf* (pl. *sharīf*) and bedouin to defect to the Sa'ūdi enemy or leave.[38] Muḥammad 'Alī claimed Ghālib's dismissal was on the sultan's instructions, and it appears he did indeed have the sultan's prior approval.[39]

After spending four days with Ṭūsūn Pasha, Ghālib found himself despatched by Muḥammad 'Alī with two of his sons and a retinue of eunuchs and servants to Jidda escorted by soldiers.[40] This escort even rifled the deposed sharīf's pockets.[41] From Jidda they sailed to al-Quṣayr, where he was met by Ibrāhīm Pasha.[42] On 1 January 1814, Burckhardt encountered the deposed sharīf there, recording: "His spirits seemed unbroken, he spoke boldly and with great dignity, but never mentioned the name either of Mohammed Aly or of his son."[43] News of the coup

[36] Ibid. vii: 143.

[37] Ibn Bishr 1982–83 i: 338. See also Mengin 1823 ii: 3–5.

[38] Al-Jabartī 1958–67 vii: 274; Burckhardt 1831 ii: 264–5.

[39] Kūrshūn 2005: 90.

[40] Al-Jabartī 1958–67 vii: 262.

[41] Ibid. vii: 267.

[42] Ibid. vii: 261.

[43] Burckhardt 1831 ii: 261.

led to the firing of cannon from the citadel in Cairo in celebration.[44] The pasha also removed the son of a previous ruling sharīf, ʿAbd Allāh ibn Surūr, from the Hijaz and kept him under house arrest in Cairo.[45] ʿAbd Allāh had spent the years 1803–1806/7 in Istanbul trying to have himself appointed ruler. On return, he applied to Imam Saʿūd in al-Dirʿiyya, who refused and detained him for three years. Once free, he posed an obvious threat to his younger brother Yaḥyā, whom the pasha had made ruling sharīf in place of his uncle Ghālib.[46] Muḥammad ʿAlī was resolved not just to uproot the Wahhābi enemy from western Arabia but to eliminate potential obstacles to his own ambitions there. Inevitably, it was not long before Yaḥyā, discovering he was a mere puppet, was complaining to the grand vizier of his treatment by Muḥammad ʿAlī and his officers in the Hijaz.[47]

Ghālib arrived in Cairo on 9 January to await "the pleasure of the Sultan".[48] This proved to be transfer to Salonica, a better fate than that envisaged by the pasha, who had advocated execution.[49] The sultan, who had received a complaint from Ghālib at his imprisonment in Cairo and restored some of his possessions to him,[50] appeared superficially to be more compassionate. But Salonica, often used by the Ottomans to park troublesome political figures, was notoriously unhealthy and prone to devastating outbreaks of the plague during summer months.[51] Exile in Salonica amounted to a death sentence. Sharīf Ghālib and his household duly died of the plague there in August 1816. His youngest son ʿAbd al-Muṭṭtalib, later ruling sharīf for three short spells, erected a domed tomb for his late father, which, though safely distant from Wahhābi levelling,

---

[44] Al-Jabartī 1958–67 vii: 257.

[45] Ibid. vii: 270. See also Burckhardt 1831 ii: 262–3.

[46] Ibn ʿAbd al-Shakūr: 556–8; Daḥlān 1887/88: 293.

[47] Letter to Muḥammad ʿAnbar of 23 November 1815, Arabic translated text in al-ʿAjlānī 1972: 258–61.

[48] Letter of Ernest Missett to Cooke of 12 January 1814 (FO 24/5) in Burdett 2013 i: 395–7, at 396. Al-Jabartī also gives 9 January as the date of arrival (1958–67 vii: 261), whereas Mengin says Ghālib arrived in Cairo on 4 December (1823 ii: 9).

[49] Kūrshūn 2005: 90.

[50] Ibn Bishr 1982–83 i: 338.

[51] Mazower 2005: 114.

was built over after 1922.[52] Ironically, in June–July 1806, in an episode that helped to reinforce the mutual distrust between the pasha and the Sublime Porte, the Ottomans had tried to transfer Muḥammad ʿAlī to Salonica as governor. He was so well entrenched in Cairo that they proved powerless to dislodge him.[53]

Muḥammad ʿAlī intervenes in the war and sidesteps the snare of peace

In October 1813, when Muḥammad ʿAlī arrived in Jidda, he expected to be away just three months.[54] He staged the coup against Ghālib and then took an active role in campaigning, without meeting the future Imam ʿAbd Allāh directly in battle. He played his part in making the war especially savage. In January 1815, after his major victory at Bisl over the Wahhābis under ʿAbd Allāh's brother Fayṣal that placed them on the defensive, he ordered the impaling of 300 prisoners, who had been previously promised quarter. Burckhardt described this as a "disgusting and atrocious act".[55] Correspondingly, the Wahhābis took no prisoners. Up to this point (1815), noted Burckhardt referring to the Wahhābis, "not a single instance is recorded of their having ever given quarter to a Turk".[56] This ruthlessness sowed terror in the opposing camp, where "discontent, and a kind of panic, were universal among the soldiers", who were ill-paid, badly supplied, and affected by the unhealthy climate.[57]

The pasha ended up being away from Cairo nearly two years. His sudden return there in June 1815 was prompted by either unfounded fears of an Ottoman attack on Alexandria, according to Burckhardt,[58] or news of Napoleon's escape from Elba and worries of a French (or British)

---

[52] De Gaury 1951: 207. See Mazower 2005: 112. ʿAbd al-Muṭṭalib (1790–1886) ruled Mecca in three spells (1827, 1851–6, 1880–81).

[53] Al-Jabartī 1958–67 vi: 288.

[54] Letter of Missett to Cooke of 14 October 1813 (FO 24/4) in Burdett 2013 i: 345–7, at 345.

[55] Burckhardt 1831 ii: 322–3 (quotation at 323).

[56] Ibid. ii: 176.

[57] Ibid. ii: 280–82 (quotation at 280).

[58] Ibid. ii: 348–9.

descent on Egypt.[59] When he reappeared, his health appeared to have been affected. People found him haughtier and less affable than before. Troops that had served with him in the Hijaz threatened insurrection at changes to their terms of service and began pillaging Cairo. The pasha, forced to retreat in haste from al-Azbakiyya in central Cairo, had to bide his time in the citadel.[60] The war was taking a heavy toll on the main Egyptian protagonists, the economy, and political stability.

Subject to acute military pressure in the al-Qaṣīm region after his father's return home, Ṭūsūn took the initiative and concluded a peace with Imam ʿAbd Allāh. The latter renounced his claim to hold the Holy Cities and declared himself subject to the sultan, in return for ready access to Mecca and al-Madīna for pilgrimage, and Ṭūsūn's evacuation of al-Qaṣīm.[61] Two Wahhābi representatives arrived in Cairo with letters for the pasha and the Sublime Porte, entering on the very day the simmering mutiny broke out among the pasha's troops.[62] One envoy was ʿAbd Allāh ibn Bunayyān, governor of al-Dirʿiyya, and the other ʿAbd al-ʿAzīz ibn Ḥamad ibn Ibrāhīm, a *qāḍī* of al-Dirʿiyya, whose maternal grandfather was Ibn ʿAbd al-Wahhāb.[63] They were accommodated with Ibrāhīm Āghā, commander of the citadel, while the pasha dealt with the insurrection.[64] If Imam ʿAbd Allāh's original intent was that the emissaries should travel on to Istanbul, the pasha and the Ottomans were unreceptive to the proposal.

The contemporary Cairene chronicler ʿAbd al-Raḥmān al-Jabartī, who interpreted the truce as ʿAbd Allāh submitting and returning to obedience to the Ottomans, describes this mission:

---

[59] Al-Jabartī 1958–67 vii: 301; Mengin 1823 ii: 48.

[60] Burckhardt 1831 ii: 350; al-Jabartī 1958–67 vii: 305–10; Belzoni 1820: 9.

[61] Burckhardt 1831 ii: 343–7.

[62] Mengin 1823 ii: 56.

[63] Ibn Bishr 1982–83 i: 378–9.

[64] Mengin 1823 ii: 57. This was a different Ibrāhīm Āghā from the former Thomas Keith, a Scots armourer of the 78th Highlanders captured in 1807, who converted, and became a hero at the taking of al-Madīna (Burckhardt 1831 ii: 240). Made governor of al-Madīna in April 1815, he was killed by the Wahhābis two months later, leading cavalry on his way to reinforce Ṭūsūn Pasha in al-Qaṣīm before Ṭūsūn proposed a peace deal. His bravery was admired by Imam ʿAbd Allāh (ibid. ii: 235, 340, 342).

> About twenty individuals from the Wahhābi community came to Ṭūsūn Pasha and two of those arrived in Cairo. The pasha [viz. Muḥammad ʿAlī] did not like this peace, showed signs of dissatisfaction with it, and did not take kindly to the appearance of the two arrivals. When they met him and he addressed them, he reproached them for their disobedience. They apologized, saying that the late Amir Masʿūd [*sic*; Saʿūd] was of a stubborn and violent disposition. He wanted an empire and to establish the [true] religion. His son, the Amir ʿAbd Allāh, on the other hand, had a mild nature and disposition. Like his late forefather, the Amir ʿAbd al-ʿAzīz, he hated the shedding of blood. He was peaceable towards the Ottoman state to the extent that there had been a close friendship between him and the late Yūsuf Pasha when he was in al-Madīna.They had not disputed or differed about anything. It was only in the days of Amir Masʿūd that the conflict had come to a head. Sharīf Ghālib was chiefly responsible for the current state of affairs, not Amir ʿAbd Allāh. The latter was of good conduct, had renounced conflict, and made the roads and routes safe for pilgrims and travellers. [They continued with] other talk designed to please. The majlis ended and they left for the place where they were ordered to reside in the company of some Turks assigned to escort them, together with their entourage, in riding here and there. They were granted permission to go wherever they wanted, so they rode up and down the streets with their entourage and escort, delighting in the town and its inhabitants. They entered al-Azhar mosque.[65]

Al-Jabartī met the visitors twice and was much taken with their manners, eloquence and learning, as well as humility and good conduct. The *qāḍī* was especially impressive and the pasha appears to have sponsored occasions when he explained Wahhābi doctrines to the local *ʿulamāʾ* and disputed with them.[66]

It is interesting that, in their desire to appear accommodating, the two Wahhābis blamed Imam Saʿūd for being hardline and presented Imam ʿAbd Allāh as almost friendly to the Ottomans. Their charges against

---

[65] Al-Jabartī 1958–67 vii: 318–19.

[66] Burckhardt 1831 ii: 351.

Sharīf Ghālib of being a troublemaker would have resonated with the pasha – and with the Ottomans, who had originally worried that Ghālib was trying to manipulate and exploit them against his petty Arabian rivals. Imam 'Abd Allāh pursued this line in an undated missive to the Sublime Porte, in which he blamed Ghālib for slandering the Wahhābis and engaging in trickery. In terms he must have found galling to use, 'Abd Allāh appealed to 'our master the sultan (*sayyidunā al-sulṭān*) Maḥmūd the Holy Warrior (*al-ghāzī*)' and undertook that from then on Sa'ūdis would obey the Ottomans. He signed the letter simply 'Abd Allāh ibn Sa'ūd.[67] His letters addressed, without further courtesies, to 'Muḥammad 'Alī Pasha', asking him to endorse the peace and then observe it, were more direct in style and less subservient in language than that directed to the Sublime Porte.[68]

That the Sa'ūdi emissaries labelled both Sa'ūd and 'Abd Allāh amir instead of *imām al-muslimīn*, the title Sa'ūd had assumed on succeeding his father 'Abd al-'Azīz, also suggests a propitiatory stance. 'Imam of the Muslims' was one of the caliph's titles. In assuming the title, which his own father had never held,[69] Sa'ūd was not making a claim to be caliph, but underlining the Wahhābis' conviction that they alone were true Muslims and their enemies were not. The pasha was familiar with this attitude. While he had been in the Hijaz, a bedouin of the 'Utayba tribe had kissed his beard and declared himself to have abandoned the religion of the Muslims (i.e. the Wahhābis) and adopted that of the heretics, the religion of Muḥammad 'Alī. Amid laughter from those present, the pasha, ever the pragmatist, had replied through his interpreter: "I hope you will always be a staunch heretic."[70]

---

[67] Undated letter, original Arabic text in 'Abd al-Raḥīm 1999: 442–5. Maḥmūd II assumed the title of '*ghāzī*' on receiving the keys to the Ka'ba in 1813 (see p. 87 below). On Ghālib, see also the undated letter of Imam 'Abd Allāh to Muḥammad 'Alī, original Arabic text in ibid.: 446–8, at 447.

[68] Undated letters of Imam 'Abd Allāh to Muḥammad 'Alī, original Arabic text in ibid.: 446–8, 449–51.

[69] *Responsum* of Shaykh 'Abd Allāh Abā Buṭayn (d. 1865) in Ibn Qāsim 1996–99 ix: 8–10, at 9. He had been a *qāḍī* of the First Sa'ūdi State.

[70] Burckhardt 1831 ii: 284–5.

Throughout the life of the First Sa'ūdi State, Wahhābi emissaries, especially *'ulamā'*, were prone to misreading the signals they received from their interlocutors. This occasion was apparently no exception. The pasha gave the visitors some money and clothes before they left.[71] They returned to Arabia, believing they had succeeded with him.[72] Yet the letter they carried from the pasha to Imam 'Abd Allāh was, according to Burckhardt, "written in a most ambiguous manner, respecting peace or war". In it the pasha demanded that the Sa'ūdis cede him al-Aḥsā', the Sa'ūdis' economically vital province in the east, as the price of confirming the agreement with Ṭūsūn.[73] This was a condition the Sa'ūdis could never accept, since they would lose their only access to the sea and would face the Ottomans on two fronts. Burckhardt's view is that either Muḥammad 'Alī, with "the contempt in which he held all engagements", or Ṭūsūn set out to deceive the Sa'ūdis. He records that, on paying a visit to his father in Alexandria in November–December 1815, Ṭūsūn was received very coldly by the pasha, presumably because of the latter's hostility to his son's peace initiative.[74]

Mengin presents a different picture. He suggests the pasha's response to the imam's letter was unambiguously condemnatory and threatening. The French text given by Mengin has the pasha accusing 'Abd Allāh of having violated his oath of obedience to 'our sovereign', bringing war to the Holy Cities, and injuring the majesty of God by stripping the Prophet's tomb. He was required to return the items taken, pass command of al-Dir'iyya to the governor of al-Madīna, and go personally to the Sublime Porte to account for his conduct. Otherwise, the pasha would send an army to chastise him.[75]

This version seems to reflect more the tough line that Muḥammad 'Alī would later adopt than the one he could afford to take at the time. He would hardly have sent such a bellicose message to al-Dir'iyya just when he needed a breathing space for his forces in Arabia to regroup and re-equip under a new commander. He also faced a dangerous

---

[71] Ibid. ii: 351.

[72] Ibn Bishr 1982–83 i: 379.

[73] Burckhardt 1831 ii: 351–2.

[74] Ibid. ii: 352–4.

[75] Mengin 1823 ii: 57.

mutiny in Cairo that threatened his very regime.[76] The vulnerability of his position was reflected in Ṭūsūn's response to the crisis. He resorted to subterfuge to maintain order and steady morale in al-Madīna before heading quickly for Cairo with some of his troops. He arrived there on 7 November to a triumphal reception that belied the ground realities of the costly war in Arabia.[77]

The menacing tone as conveyed by Mengin would have fatally compromised Ṭūsūn's credibility and authority as peacemaker at this delicate moment, something the pasha would have been loath to do to the son whom, by all accounts, he loved the most. The Sa'ūdis would have realised immediately that this was a fight to the death, instead of deluding themselves for a period that they had reached some kind of temporary accommodation with the pasha. According to the Sa'ūdi chronicler, in 1815/16 Imam 'Abd Allāh sent a second mission to the pasha in Cairo with gifts and letters confirming the peace, but the delegation found Muḥammad 'Alī had changed his stance and was accusing the imam of breaching the truce.[78]

One of the conditions for a lasting peace that Muḥammad 'Alī, when in the Hijaz, had previously set in an open letter to Imam 'Abd Allāh, with no expectation of Wahhābi acceptance and recognising it was now impossible to fulfil, was the return of the treasures from the Prophet's tomb.[79] According to Mengin, after the pasha wrote threateningly to Imam 'Abd Allāh, the latter replied that nothing remained of the treasures taken by his father. Everything had been sold and dissipated.[80] That the Wahhābis could not rectify their sacrilege, as the pasha saw it, encouraged him to keep the spotlight on an episode that had provoked so much popular upset and seemed to symbolise their irreligious attitude.

---

[76] In a report datelined Constantinople 1 August 1817 (i.e. much later), *The Times* reported: "Two couriers have arrived here from the Pacha of Egypt, with news of a victory over the Wechabites, and several sacks filled with ears according to the Turkish practice. This victory is not important, but it proves the unfounded nature of the rumours which were spread about the revolt at Cairo and the deposition and imprisonment of the Pacha."

[77] Mengin 1823 ii: 58–9.

[78] Ibn Bishr 1982–83 i: 383.

[79] Burckhardt 1831 ii: 336.

[80] Mengin 1823 ii: 67.

It stood high on the Ottomans' charge sheet as an offence against God and His Prophet that demanded retribution. In terms of condemning the Wahhābis, it had the virtues of simplicity and notoriety, was easy to prove, and had deep resonance among both elites and the common people across the Islamic world.

Muḥammad 'Alī may have been dangerously placed in late 1815, but a lasting agreement with the Sa'ūdis would not have been in his interests. He was ready to profit from an extended truce to prepare his final campaign to crush 'Abd Allāh and his followers, but he knew the Wahhābis would prove fickle partners in any longer-term peace. They would be driven by their religious creed to seek the recovery of the Holy Cities from infidel occupiers, and it was inevitable over time that they would seek to undermine their enemies' control of the ground and populace, especially the powerful tribes around the Holy Cities. Shaykh 'Abd al-Raḥmān ibn Ḥasan indeed later acknowledged that, pursuant to God's Will, Imam 'Abd Allāh had breached the agreement by demanding the allegiance of southern tribes, sparking the pasha's anger.[81]

The pasha was resolved to drive the campaign to a decisive conclusion. He did not want to become enmeshed in an endless anti-Wahhābi counter-insurgency campaign in the harsh terrain of the Hijaz borderlands. He knew that, with the Holy Cities returned to Ottoman sovereignty, there was a risk the sultan might settle for a half-victory that amounted to no more than a stalemate. It might even suit the Sublime Porte for the over-mighty governor of Egypt to be bogged down indefinitely in a conflict that would sap his military strength and popularity, as he tried to hold the line around the Holy Cities. Muḥammad 'Alī had no wish to fall into this trap. He had to see his enemies in al-Dir'iyya destroyed, and was ready to commit all his resources to this goal. In the event, he succeeded with a conventional military campaign, but then spent twenty years trying unsuccessfully to pacify Central Arabia. Finally, in a curious codicil to the Imam 'Abd Allāh story, he resorted to one of the imam's younger brothers to help shore up Egyptian rule in Najd – an experiment that failed.

---

[81] 'Abd al-Raḥmān Āl al-Shaykh 2005: 123–4.

CHAPTER 4

The Pasha's Second Arabian Campaign and the Fall of al-Dir'iyya

Ibrāhīm Pasha's offensive

Muḥammad 'Alī's final expeditionary campaign of 1816–18 in the sultan's name was a relentless slog across Arabia. He entrusted command to his brutally effective and ruthless son Ibrāhīm in succession to the relatively mild-mannered Ṭūsūn. Recalled by his father, the latter died of the plague in Rosetta in 1816, apparently infected by a slave girl who was said to have entranced him.[1]

After a tough campaign from Yanbu' to al-Dir'iyya, via al-Madīna, al-Qaṣīm, al-Washm and Ḍurmā, that subjected Najd to its first-ever foreign invasion, Ibrāhīm arrived before the Sa'ūdi capital in March 1818 and began to tighten the noose around it in April.[2] This advance, punctuated by protracted sieges and massacres, such as the one at Ḍurmā in late February 1818 that saw the death of over 1,200 inhabitants at the hands of rampaging Ottoman forces, was made possible by Ibrāhīm's attention to logistics and the support of large tribes such as the Ḥarb and Muṭayr, which had deserted the Wahhābi cause.

Although the Sa'ūdis continued to resist strongly, their state and its regime of godliness proved more brittle than they, and others, had expected. It disintegrated with surprising speed. Imam 'Abd Allāh

[1] Forbin 1819: 310–11. De Forbin himself made an apparently unsuccessful auction bid for a beautiful young slave girl in Cairo (ibid.: 233–4).

[2] A popular account of the campaign appears in Facey 1997: 64–76.

probably made the situation worse by retreating too soon to al-Dirʿiyya, instead of pursuing a strategy of harrying Ibrāhīm's supply lines, which would have played to Saʿūdi military strengths. The loyalty of the bedouin was always conditional. Once subject to Ibrāhīm's blandishments and immune to Saʿūdi pressure and reprisal, many tribes switched sides with alacrity. Imam ʿAbd Allāh had prepared al-Dirʿiyya's defences, but there were weak points that Ibrāhīm had the artillery and expertise to exploit. The Saʿūdis were not well organised, equipped or trained for set-piece conventional warfare.

Ibrāhīm still suffered setbacks. A major reverse occurred on 23 June 1818, even as he had victory within his grasp. His army's main ammunition store exploded. An Italian doctor with his forces described it as one of the greatest explosions he had ever heard, even though he was a kilometre away. All the tents collapsed, and sixty or seventy caught fire, while seventeen men were killed.[3] The Saʿūdi chronicler says the sound carried the distance of "three or four days' travel" and destroyed men, horses, food and materiel. This devastation caused him to wonder why the Wahhābis did not exploit the sudden weakness of the Ottomans and the psychological advantage offered by the explosion to raid them in their tents.[4] The Ottoman historian, however, recorded that "the Imperial Army suffered considerable losses due to a quick succession of concentrated attacks by the Wahhābis".[5] Though desperately short of food and ammunition, Ibrāhīm regrouped and stood firm. He assembled ammunition from al-Madīna and neighbouring towns, and demanded, and received, urgent reinforcements and resupplies from Cairo.[6] Caravans streamed in, some arranged by anti-Wahhābi exiles in al-Zubayr and Basra. They sent crucial provisions, including rice, wheat and tobacco, and the materiel that Ibrāhīm now desperately needed (and for which he presumably paid).[7] Resupplied, Ibrāhīm re-intensified the siege.

---

[3] Letter of Andrea Gentili to Drovetti, summarised in Ridley n.d.: 78.

[4] Ibn Bishr 1982–83 i: 411. See also Mengin's criticism (1823 ii: 142).

[5] Cevdet 1874 xi: 57.

[6] Letter to his father of 24 June 1818, Arabic translation of the text in al-ʿAjlānī 1972: 205–9, at 208–9 (this translation is obviously bowdlerised).

[7] Ibn Bishr 1982–83 i: 411.

Sa'ūdi capitulation

Eventually, Ibrāhīm Pasha's forces overcame the dogged Sa'ūdi defence organised by Imam 'Abd Allāh. Successive bastions, gun emplacements and towers succumbed to the invaders, as they moved down the ribbon valley of Wadi Ḥanīfa and gradually choked the remaining defenders. Al-Dir'iyya finally fell on 11 September 1818. The months of siege had inflicted heavy losses on both sides. One estimate was that, of the people of al-Dir'iyya and environs, 1,300 died. These included twenty-one men from the Āl Sa'ūd, among them Fayṣal and Ibrāhīm, brothers of the imam, as well as various of his cousins and members of lesser branches of the clan. This was evidence enough, observes the Sa'ūdi chronicler, of the Āl Sa'ūd's direct engagement in the fighting. There were heavy losses too among families closely associated with them, such as the Āl Mu'ammar of al-'Uyayna, from whom Imam Sa'ūd's mother came.[8] These casualties, as well his personal responsibility for a failed defensive strategy, would have weighed heavily on Imam 'Abd Allāh's state of mind as the siege entered its final stages.

In the last days, as he experienced the acute loneliness of a defeated commander, Imam 'Abd Allāh did not even have the counsel and support of the Āl al-Shaykh. A few days before, Ibn 'Abd al-Wahhāb's elderly son, 'Abd Allāh, head of the religious establishment, had drawn his sword to rally the defenders of the Āl al-Shaykh quarter of al-Bujayrī across the wadi from the Āl Sa'ūd quarter of al-Ṭurayf where the imam was based. Despite some success against the enemy, on 7 September Imam 'Abd Allāh's uncle 'Abd Allāh and Shaykh 'Alī ibn Muḥammad ibn 'Abd al-Wahhāb were forced to visit Ibrāhīm Pasha under truce to sue for peace. The latter insisted that Imam 'Abd Allāh and the last pockets of Wahhābi resistance surrender to him.[9]

After the final battle, in which he was encircled from all sides on the al-Ṭurayf promontory on the west side of the wadi, Imam 'Abd Allāh found himself suddenly deserted by many of his followers, allegedly bribed by the enemy.[10] This marked the collapse of all hope for the beleaguered leader. He was now faced imminently with an outcome that, for all his

---

[8] Ibid. i: 418–20.

[9] Ibid. i: 416–17.

[10] Ibid. i: 417.

faith, must have long appeared inexorable as, week by week, day by day, the area under his control in the Wadi Ḥanīfa had shrunk. He knew that further resistance not only was futile, but would forfeit any remaining chance of protecting his family and people. There was to be no last-hour reprieve from God, no recovery, no miraculous turning of the tables, only the enactment of God's will in favour of al-Dir'iyya's destruction by troops the Wahhābis had taunted as 'polytheists'.

On 9 September, Ibrāhīm Pasha told Sa'ūdi representatives suing for peace on the imam's behalf that the imam had to present himself in person. Two days later, 'Abd Allāh emerged from the ruins of the Āl Sa'ūd quarter of al-Dir'iyya and submitted.[11] Ibrāhīm stipulated, and 'Abd Allāh had little option but to accept, that the latter should travel to Maḥmūd II for the sultan to deal with him as he wished.[12] Mengin records that 'Abd Allāh asked for his life to be spared. He says that Ibrāhīm, impressed by 'Abd Allāh's demeanour, declined to give an assurance on that score. This would be to presume the wishes of his father and the sultan. He was sure they were too generous to kill him.[13] Given the history of political and religious hostility between Ottomans and Wahhābis, 'Abd Allāh can have had few illusions himself. He surely knew, and accepted, that his life was forfeit the moment he committed himself to travel to Istanbul.

Imam 'Abd Allāh leaves al-Dir'iyya for Cairo

After an interval of two days, Ibrāhīm Pasha told Imam 'Abd Allāh to prepare for his journey.[14] Ibrāhīm deputed two senior figures, the *duwaydār* ('trusted attendant')[15] and Rashwān Āghā, who had been one of his senior commanders during the last stages of the campaign, each with their troops, to accompany him.[16] The military escort was sizeable, around 400

[11] Ibid. i: 417. Mengin's account is slightly different at 1823 ii: 132–3. He suggests that Imam 'Abd Allāh met Ibrāhīm in person on 9 September and, on being told he was to be sent to Egypt on Muḥammad 'Alī's instructions, asked for another twenty-four hours to reflect on final surrender.

[12] Ibn Bishr 1982–83 i: 417.

[13] Mengin 1823 ii: 134.

[14] Ibn Bishr 1982–83 i: 421.

[15] According to Ottoman records, this was Ḥusayn Āghā (al-Qaḥṭānī 2010: 276, n. 1).

[16] Ibn Bishr 1982–83 i: 421–2.

infantry.[17] This was to prevent 'Abd Allāh fleeing; deter Wahhābi rescue attempts; and safeguard from marauding bedouin or thieving soldiery the treasure, booty and despatches Ibrāhīm Pasha was sending home. Wrenched from the capital he had just surrendered, the defeated imam set off for Cairo on an apparently uneventful two-month journey by land, via al-Madīna, to Yanbu' and then by sea to Suez.[18] This was certainly the longest sea journey 'Abd Allāh had ever experienced. It may even have been his first, since in the Gulf and Red Sea the Wahhābis had relied on maritime surrogates, especially the Qawāsim of Rās al-Khayma, to support their land campaigns, and had no naval forces of their own.

The imam had for company 'Abd Allāh al-Sirrī and 'Abd al-'Azīz ibn Salmān, described by Mengin (and Bowes Wright) as respectively his treasurer and his secretary, but in reality of lesser rank.[19] The Ottoman interrogators later reported 'Abd al-'Azīz as describing himself as the assistant secretary to the imam and 'Abd Allāh al-Sirrī as saying he was the imam's personal servant and valet.[20] Both attended his session with Muḥammad 'Alī in Cairo and shared his fate in Istanbul. Mengin also reports slaves accompanying the imam to Cairo.[21] The party had custody of a metal box that Imam Sa'ūd had entrusted with a record of its contents to the safekeeping of his daughter (and 'Abd Allāh's sister) Mūḍī in al-Dir'iyya.[22] According to 'Abd Allāh's valet under questioning in Istanbul, the imam's brother 'Abd al-Raḥmān had brought it to 'Abd Allāh, while he was sitting with Ibrāhīm after the surrender, and told him

---

17 Mengin 1823 ii: 134–5.

18 Imam 'Abd Allāh's party arrived in Cairo from the Suez direction accompanied by the *Qubṭān* of Suez, so this was presumably where he landed in Egypt.

19 Mengin 1823 ii: 134.

20 Zaydān 1975: 185. The Russian embassy in Istanbul described them inaccurately as 'Abd Allāh's minister and (personal) imam (i.e. cleric) (Vassiliev 1998: 155).

21 Mengin 1823 ii: 134. Ibn Bishr says three or four men only made up 'Abd Allāh's entourage (1982–83 i: 421). However, 'Abd al-'Azīz told his Ottoman interrogators that twelve in all of 'Abd Allāh's servants went with him to Cairo. There the pasha had permitted only two, chosen by 'Abd Allāh, to travel on with him to Istanbul. 'Abd al-'Azīz added that he and his companion had been gratified to be chosen, unaware of what lay in store for them (Zaydān 1975: 185).

22 Muḍīfa is the name as given in the original Ottoman document (ibid.: 186), but this is probably a corruption of Mūḍī (my thanks to Dr Saud al-Sarhan for pointing this out).

to take it, since the Ottomans would ask him about the contents. The imam had then presented the box to Ibrāhīm.[23]

Ibrāhīm Pasha stayed behind in al-Dir'iyya for nine more months, levelling the town, imposing Egyptian control on Najd and al-Aḥsā', and sending batches of Āl Sa'ūd and Āl al-Shaykh (descendants of Ibn 'Abd al-Wahhāb) to Cairo with their families.[24] Sources conflict on what, if any, undertakings Ibrāhīm gave Imam 'Abd Allāh on his capitulation to spare the town, the people and their property. Mengin certainly believed that 'Abd Allāh requested and received assurances for the safety of his family, the preservation of al-Dir'iyya, and immunity for those who had fought against Ibrāhīm's forces.[25] Irrespective, with characteristic ruthlessness, Ibrāhīm dismantled al-Dir'iyya, tortured and killed selected prisoners (while apparently treating most members of the Āl Sa'ūd well), and plundered surrounding areas.[26] This was presumably on his father's orders, although Ibrāhīm later told a British emissary, George Sadleir, that the order for levelling al-Dir'iyya came from the sultan, not his father.[27] Sadleir noted:

> The walls which surrounded the town, the forts and several houses have been razed. The Pacha [Ibrāhīm] was determined to render this spot a wilderness and previous to his departure caused the date plantations and gardens to be destroyed. At the present moment there is not a single family inhabiting its ruins ....[28]

The Sa'ūdi chronicler implies that Ibrāhīm launched his reprisals, including against clerics, even before the imam's departure, whereas

---

[23] Zaydān 1975: 185.

[24] Ibn Bishr 1982–83 i: 430–2. See further Chapter 9 below.

[25] Mengin 1823 ii: 134. Shaykh 'Abd al-Raḥmān ibn Ḥasan, a *muftī* and *qāḍī* of al-Dir'iyya in 1818, remained convinced that Ibrāhīm gave such undertakings (2005: 128). Yet the reliable Sa'ūdi chronicler Ibn Bishr does not mention them (1982–83 i: 417–18).

[26] According to Cevdet, the sultan told Muḥammad 'Alī it was up to him how he chose to neutralise al-Dir'iyya (1874 xi: 58).

[27] Sadleir 1866: 83.

[28] Sadleir 1866: 75. Contained in a letter addressed to Bombay Governor Sir Evan Nepean, Sadleir's reference to 'wilderness' is an apposite nod to Tacitus's *Agricola* and his famous Latin dictum on the Roman occupation of Britain: "Where they make a wilderness, they call it peace" ("ubi solitudinem faciunt, pacem appellant").

Mengin suggests he did not.[29] If 'Abd Allāh ever learned the extent of the trauma Ibrāhīm inflicted on his homeland, the news would have come from the Ottomans on his arrival in Istanbul. Ibrāhīm himself did not see Cairo again until 9 December 1819, when he was greeted with official celebrations.[30] As Muḥammad 'Alī's scribe told an exiled Wahhābi, 12,000 men who left Cairo to fight in Arabia never returned.[31]

The view from Cairo

If Central Arabia endured tough times during the war and now faced the trauma of decades of political turbulence, feuding, and social and economic disruption, the common people in Cairo and across Egypt had long experienced hardship and deprivation. This was caused in part by the costs of the pasha's Arabian war. As early as August 1814, nearly half-way through the campaign, the British Consul-General in Cairo, Ernest Missett, coming to the end of a long and controversial career in Egypt, wrote succinctly to London:

> Certain it is, that the resources of the people are nearly exhausted, and that it will be impossible for them to bear much longer the burthens under which they labour; and though their patience is naturally almost unconquerable, yet so oppressive are the financial measures lately adopted, that there would be every reason to apprehend a general insurrection, had not the Viceroy removed every individual either able or disposed to become the leader of the malcontents.[32]

Writing about the end of the war in 1818, al-Jabartī was explicit about its dire impact on the Egyptian economy over many years. The provisioning

---

29 Ibn Bishr 1982– 3 i: 421; Mengin 1823 ii: 136.

30 Al-Jabartī 1958–67 vii: 459–60. Ibrāhīm's triumphant homecoming was marred a few weeks later by the death of his six-year-old son (ibid. vii: 460–1). See also Mengin 1823 ii: 189–90.

31 Ibn Bishr 1982–83 i: 418. At this stage of the pasha's rule, relatively few of those would have been locals, as the pasha's army comprised mainly Turks, Albanians, Moroccans and other non-Egyptians. The initial Egyptian army had consisted of 8,000 men (Marsot 1984: 200).

32 Letter of Missett to Cooke of 5 August 1814 (FO 24/5) in Burdett 2013 i: 412–14, at 414.

of the expeditionary army with food, ammunition and other supplies, and their transportation across Arabia, had imposed extraordinary costs.[33] The longer the war went on, the longer the supply lines, and the more inhospitable the terrain, the higher the taxes imposed by the pasha.[34]

News of the battle for al-Dir'iyya had filtered through from Arabia, partly in the form of despatches from Ibrāhīm Pasha to his father, some of which he forwarded to Istanbul.[35] On 5 May 1818, Cairenes learnt that Ibrāhīm had taken part of the capital and boxed in the Wahhābis.[36] Reports followed of setbacks at Wahhābi hands, including the explosion of the ammunition stores in late June. By early September the pasha, aware that his son was close to victory, was on tenterhooks, sponsoring readings and prayers at al-Azhar. Agitated and fed up with waiting for news, he shifted restlessly around Cairo from the citadel to his Shubrā Palace, then al-Āthār Palace, al-Azbakiyya, al-Gīza, and so on.[37] His anxiety allegedly even triggered an eye inflammation.[38] Finally, on 8 October came news, via 'Uthmān Āghā al-Wardānī, amir of Yanbu', that Ibrāhīm Pasha had taken al-Dir'iyya and subdued the Wahhābis.[39]

The pasha was ecstatic. Batteries of cannon began firing from the citadel, al-Gīza, Būlāq, and al-Azbakiyya in celebration. Five days later, official despatches confirming the tidings triggered renewed cannonades in late afternoon that lasted hours, with a thousand firings from the citadel, and coincided with the fireworks for 'Īd al-Aḍḥā'.[40] The pasha ordered extended celebrations from 28 October, when the firework displays that were to last until 3 November started with the thunder of the quick firing

---

33 Al-Jabartī 1958–67 vii: 433–4.

34 As with the increase in land tax (*kharāj*) introduced by the pasha in 1818 to help pay for the war (ibid. vii: 436).

35 Examples of such despatches are in Ibn Khamīs 1982: first appendix: 1–16.

36 Al-Jabartī 1958 –67 vii: 429.

37 Ibid. vii: 431–2.

38 Mengin 1823 ii: 135.

39 Al-Jabartī 1958–67 vii: 432.

40 Ibid. Mengin says the news arrived from Yanbu' on 18 October. The official despatches may have been those carried by Muḥammad Effendi, Ibrāhīm's secretary (1823 ii: 135). See also the letter from Sayyid Aḥmad Adīb, *kiḥyā* of the grand vizier, to Muḥammad 'Alī of 24 November 1818 in 'Abd al-Raḥīm 1983: 673–5.

of cannon in the European style.[41] Hurriedly the pasha dispatched two messengers, whom he rewarded handsomely with sable pelts and cash, to carry the news to Istanbul.[42] Their arrival there on 19 November set off three days of public celebrations, with cannons fired from fortresses and towers surrounding the Ottoman capital three times a day.[43] The pasha's representative in Istanbul wrote to him on 22 November relating how the Ottomans at all levels were delighted by the news of al-Dir'iyya's capture and the seizure of Imam 'Abd Allāh alive.[44] On 20 November, the British embassy in Istanbul noted both the 'highest importance' of the victory to Sultan Maḥmūd in settling the future of the Holy Cities, and the sultan's instruction for the prisoners to be delivered to the Ottoman capital to await his verdict on their fate.[45]

Despite harsh living conditions and a daily struggle to make ends meet, the people of Cairo made the most of the festivities, which resumed on the Nile's banks on 9 November and lasted until 16 November.[46] Cooking oils, bread and other necessities were in short supply. Whatever meat there was, from emaciated sheep, was bad. When the authorities released wheat supplies from the pasha's warehouses for sale, they were found to be contaminated with worm. People complained, yet still set out to enjoy themselves. Shops stayed open all day and all night.[47] Unconscious of the daily realities for ordinary Cairenes, new arrivals John Bowes Wright and his companions were struck by this festive aspect. Astonished, the former would write:

---

[41] Al-Jabartī 1958–67 vii: 432, 443–4. He offers a detailed description of the displays at ibid. vii: 443-4.

[42] Kūrshūn 2005: 93, n. 285. The messengers did well, as the sultan also rewarded them (letter of Muḥammad Najīb to Muḥammad 'Alī of 22 November 1818 in 'Abd al-Raḥīm 1983: 670–2). The facsimile of the sultan's order is at Kūrshūn 2005: appendix, unpaginated.

[43] Cevdet 1874 xi: 58.

[44] Letter of Muḥammad Najīb to Muḥammad 'Alī of 22 November 1818 in 'Abd al-Raḥīm 1983: 670–2, as confirmed by Kiḥyā Adīb's letter of 24 November at ibid.: 674. See also Kūrshūn 2005: 93.

[45] Unsigned letter to Foreign Secretary Lord Castlereagh of 23 November 1818 (FO 195/22) in Burdett 2013 i: 548–9.

[46] Al-Jabartī 1958–67 vii: 445–6.

[47] Ibid. vii: 432–3.

> As we approached Boulack, the Port of Cairo and about two miles from it, after dark, we perceived the most brilliant illuminations and fireworks .... We could not possibly have visited this capital at a more favourable juncture, indeed I doubt if old Father Nile has witnessed such doings since the splendid days of the Pharaohs or Cleopatras [*sic*].[48]

It was highly fortuitous that the small group of Englishmen should have sailed into Cairo at this precise moment, catching the end of the festivities and making themselves witnesses to a political occasion of major regional significance.

[48] Letter of 18 November 1818, from Cairo.

CHAPTER 5

The English Whig

John Bowes Wright

John Bowes Wright (1779–1836) was born into a landowning family in Durham, the second son of a lawyer. He grew up in Newcastle upon Tyne and was educated first at Edinburgh University, where he formed an intimate friendship with a fellow Northumbrian undergraduate, Joseph Lamb (1781–1859), one of three brothers from a prominent family in Newcastle.[1] In 1802, Bowes Wright went on to Jesus College, Cambridge, where he is said to have excelled in classics and modern languages.[2] Four years later, he was elected a permanent Fellow of the college, although this does not seem to have imposed any teaching obligations of any kind in return for the fluctuating emoluments he received.[3] He was called to the Bar at Lincoln's Inn in 1813, though he never appears to have practised law. When in England, he spent time in London and Cambridge and resided in the house built by his father in Queen's Square, Newcastle.[4]

Jesus College had sixteen Foundation Fellows, fifteen representing an English county and one Wales.[5] Six of these were required to be in holy

---

[1] Background on Joseph Lamb is contained in Lamb 1926: 64–127.

[2] Venn 1954 Pt II vi: 595. He became a member of Jesus in 1802.

[3] Certificate of admission to a fellowship at Jesus College, Cambridge, of John Bowes Wright, dated 15 April 1806 is in Northumberland Archives, NRO 2659/41. Various documents relating to Bowes Wright form part of the Lamb Family Papers held by Northumberland Archives, ref. NRO 2659/1–100.

[4] Welford 1895 iii: 686.

[5] Anon. 1833: 277.

orders. Bowes Wright, who represented Northumberland, was not one of them, although he is occasionally styled the Rev. John Bowes Wright, despite the absence of any record that he studied divinity or was ordained into the clergy. Indeed, his letters are strikingly free of religious sentiment, any sense of personal religious faith, and all mention of regular church-going, although this did not stop him doing religious sightseeing on the continent and in 1817 contriving to be presented to the pope.[6] This indifference to religion was consistent with his stance as a Whig.

As Leslie Mitchell has observed, "it was generally held that to offer religion to a Whig was the equivalent of offering garlic to a vampire. … [Whigs] were not so much against religion as oblivious to it."[7] They opposed proselytising and missionaries and advocated religious toleration. "Inevitably, few Whigs believed that religion should be the principal regulator of private morality",[8] while Whig historians viewed "the main purpose of religious creeds" as justifying "men in slaughtering their fellows. Every doctrinal dispute easily transmuted into massacre and persecution."[9] Bowes Wright's correspondence betrays little interest in the tenets of Wahhābism (or in Islam generally). His instincts would have been out of sympathy with the movement, not because he was a strong Christian, but because he would have been repelled by both its regime of godliness and its harsh campaign against other Muslims. The perpetual conflict between the Wahhābis and their opponents would have confirmed to him that Whig historians were right about the slaughter sparked by religion.

Bowes Wright chose not to reside in Cambridge, yet continued to draw his Fellow's salary. When abroad, he remained in touch with Cambridge affairs principally through his friend the Rev. George Adam Browne (1774–1843), who seems to have arranged the payment of Bowes Wright's Fellow's 'dividends'. Browne, who was made senior Fellow of Trinity in 1823, became chaplain to the Duke of Sussex. The latter was the sixth son of George III. Cast out by the Royal Family for marrying

---

6 Letter of 24 May 1817, from Rome. Bowes Wright's final letter to Joseph Lamb of 25 January 1836, when he knew he might soon die, does not mention God or religion, although he expressed a wish to be buried with his parents in Tynemouth Priory.

7 Mitchell 2007: 117.

8 Ibid.: 121.

9 Ibid.: 123.

twice contrary to the Royal Marriage Act 1772, he had established an independent court at Kensington Palace. Sussex was also the most senior Freemason in the country. For thirty years (1813–43) he served as Grand Master of the United Grand Lodge of England, which was created when two Grand Lodges combined in 1813 (he had succeeded his brother the Prince Regent, later King George IV, in one of the roles). By virtue of his post with Sussex, Browne was a Freemason of some influence, even though Freemasonry, as a development of the Enlightenment, was entirely secular in character.[10] Bowes Wright too was a Freemason. This gave him a useful network during his travels, although not in Ottoman society. More research is required into whether the lodges reportedly founded in Egypt by the invading French forces in the years 1798–1801, which had involved some collaborationist Egyptian elements, remained active among Egyptians once the French withdrew.[11] There is some evidence that one-time French consul Bernardino Drovetti was a leading light in keeping the movement alive in Egypt.[12]

Although Bowes Wright could rely for income on investments and considerable property in the Newcastle area, it was his payments from Cambridge that funded many of his travels from 1801 onwards. Over the next three decades he was the quintessential Grand Tourist on the continent. In the Near East, he showed himself to be a proper traveller rather than a mere tourist,[13] ready to undergo the rigours of camelback, local watercraft and bandit country. It helped that he was an excellent linguist. Unlike some of his more exhibitionist fellow countrymen who travelled in the Eastern Mediterranean or Near East, such as the famous poet Lord Byron (d. 1824) and James Silk Buckingham (d. 1855), he did not seek to immortalise himself in portraits wearing exotic local costumes. That he had no direct descendants, spent much of his life on the move, and seems from his correspondence to have been free of personal vanity or ego may explain why there does not seem to be an extant portrait of him.

---

[10] Hogg 2012: 30, 34, 61. He sponsored the induction of Belzoni into a Cambridge Lodge in 1821.

[11] See Landau 1965: 139; Wissa 1989: 145. Muḥammad ʿAlī's youngest son ʿAbd al-Ḥalīm became Egypt's leading Freemason in 1845.

[12] Galtier 2006: *passim*.

[13] A useful and important distinction analysed by Fussell 1980: 37–50.

Bowes Wright as correspondent, traveller and partisan Whig

Bowes Wright's letters home, addressing as "my dear Joe" his friend Joseph Lamb, who remained tied to home by marriage, family and expanding business interests (he was to become mayor of Newcastle in 1837) form a remarkable archive of the Grand Tour era from 1802 onwards. They offer a detailed diary of travel during the years 1801–1832 that deserves full publication. Long, colourful, packed with incident and adorned with the classical erudition typical of the day, they express eloquently the educated Whig sensibility of the time with its bias in favour of constitutional monarchy, civil and religious freedom, extended suffrage, the abolition of slavery, and free trade. They reveal their author to have been a skilled observer of people and customs, scenery and sights, with an awareness of social and political conditions doubtless sharpened by his command of French and Italian, as he went about "everywhere deeply studying men and manners, and scattering, as opportunity offered, the seeds of public liberty, to which he was passionately attached".[14] These traits are to be found recorded in the choir of the ruined Tynemouth Priory, where he was buried in February 1836. This contains "tablets to the memory of the Wrights, on which the scholarship, the enterprise, and the liberal views of John Bowes Wright are set forth in elegant Latin".[15]

Bowes Wright was able to mix easily with the upper echelons of society wherever he went, aided by letters of introduction, an expanding list of personal contacts, Freemasonry links, and highly favourable exchange rates for British currency. Following the Napoleonic wars, the British were mostly popular and sought-after, although those travellers who left debts behind were damaging their reputation, according to Bowes Wright in 1816.[16] Many educated Englishmen lived abroad permanently and cheaply, often with their wives and families. Joseph Lamb's own brother, Humble Lamb, also a close friend of Bowes Wright, moved to Switzerland

---

[14] Welford 1895 iii: 686, quoting William Brockie's *The Family Names of the Folks of Shields* (1857) 83.

[15] Ibid. iii: 686 (viz. "Diversas civitates diversa hominum ingenia curiosius exploravit, strenuus ubique liberates publicae vindex"). Joseph Lamb was Bowes Wright's sole executor (final letter of 25 January 1836) and the beneficiary of the residue of his estate, including personal effects (final will and testament of Bowes Wright of 13 January 1836).

[16] Letter of 24 August 1816, from Frankfurt-am-Main ("a very dear and disagreeable town").

with his children after his wife died young in 1819, living so long there that he became known as the 'squire of Vevey'. Bowes Wright frequently urged Joseph to accompany him on his adventures, to enjoy "visiting the wonders, and sojourning among the noble citizens of the world, men who despise the differences of place and education, but see in all something to please and to admire".[17]

Joseph opted instead for marriage (to a Catholic), family and burgeoning business interests, including collieries and railways, the Tyne Bank and the Northumberland Glassworks. It was the building of this commercial empire that prevented Lamb from joining Bowes Wright on his many travels, although he did accompany him twice, on journeys in France and Italy in 1814, while Napoleon was on Elba, and in 1824, just after Lamb had married. Bowes Wright himself never married. He regarded constancy as boring and associated marriage with "chains". He was determined not to "be shackled in my expeditions" and prevented from indulging his wanderlust.[18] He told Joe: "Should I ever marry, it will not be for some time yet; I must see more countries and follow the dictates of my naturally wandering disposition."[19] Yet he was a connoisseur of female beauty and much enjoyed female company and dancing, as his letters make clear. These allude to regular, if fleeting, dalliances with ladies of varying nationalities and backgrounds.

"Whiggery cannot be understood in an English context alone. Travel, intellect and curiosity led them to admire other cultures and pre-eminently that of France. Francophilia was every Whig's opportunity and birthright. For many, Paris was more of a second home than the country house."[20] Bowes Wright fitted firmly into this pattern. He was a strong Francophile, like many of his own immediate circle, including Joseph Lamb (who sometimes addressed him 'Mon cher Le Droit'). His letters over many years display a marked preference for 'lively' Paris, which he visited regularly, over dull London. Like many Whigs, including famously Lord and Lady Holland, Bowes Wright displayed considerable sympathy for

---

[17] Letter of 31 January 1815, from Paris.

[18] Letter of 7 March 1818, from Rome.

[19] Letter of 19 February 1823, from Paris. It was only in 1831, five years before his death, that he observed: "I begin to tire of having no fixed place where to lay my head" (letter of 30 July 1831, from Paris).

[20] Mitchell 2007: 77.

Napoleon. He had hoped to visit the deposed emperor on Elba in 1815, relying on letters of introduction to Napoleon's minister there, Count Bertrand, including from Captain Usher who had helped to convey the party there.[21] He was in Paris in March 1815 when Napoleon escaped from Elba ("France is in a quiver from one end of it to the other"[22]), and managed to leave the city a week before Napoleon's arrival on 20 March.[23] "Quel homme étonnant and terrible who can thus by his mere presence fill the world with alarm!!", he remarked.[24] "This is a pretty sequel to follow [Foreign Secretary] Lord Castlereagh's annunciation of the glorious labours of the Congress [of Vienna] and universal pacification," he declared, wondering whether the British had precipitated Napoleon's departure from Elba by threatening to send him to St Helena, in breach of their treaty with him.[25]

Initially, he noted "the English are believed to have facilitated the event, not only by the lower orders but by the more respectable part of the community" in order to create civil war in France.[26] Paris was soon in ferment and, once safely back in London, he remarked on "the hostile and evil spirit that unequivocally displayed itself against the English" that had driven him to leave the French capital. "It became evident that should there be popular commotion the English would be first to fall victims."[27] He and his companions were subject to verbal abuse from army units, some of whose soldiers wanted to bayonet them, but they escaped unscathed, via Arras, to Calais, and then Dover. Yet London appeared "'triste' and stupid after the lively scenes of Paris", which he regretted leaving.[28] "If there is anything like a truce, I shall instantly return. I find England dull and stupid to a degree, the theatres

---

[21] Letter of 29 January 1815, from Paris.

[22] Letter of 10 February 1815, from Paris.

[23] Letter of 12 March 1815, from Paris ("The aspect of affairs here is most gloomy and terrific").

[24] Letter of 10 February 1815, from Paris.

[25] Letter of 11 February 1815, from Paris.

[26] Letter of 11 February 1815, from Paris. See also letter of 10 February 1815, from Paris.

[27] Letter of 22 March 1815, from London.

[28] Ibid.

incomparably below those of Paris."[29] He also preferred French dances, including waltzing and 'contre-danses', to those of the English, which the French considered "outré and ungraceful".[30] He relished French satirical portrayals of his own countrymen. In January 1815, he observed that: "They have brought out a capital thing at the Variétés, 'Les Anglais pour rire', where Potier and Brunet as the disguised Anglaises afford the French infinite amusement; they also burlesque and English country dance with great success."[31]

Before the battle of Waterloo in June 1815, the Duke of Sussex opined to Bowes Wright that a new war would ruin the country and he intended to raise his voice loudly against it in Parliament. He considered that Viscount Castlereagh ought to lose his head. Bowes Wright himself declared: "I hope the country will not be so stupidly lost, as to suffer the imbecile fools who rule us, to plunge us into a new war." His sympathy for Napoleon misled him into asserting that "all the world united cannot dethrone him". In his view, France was at this point (i.e. just before Waterloo) "stronger than she has been since the campaign of Russia and an invading army would be discomfited and destroyed".[32]

In France in August 1816, he reflected on the price of Waterloo:

> Throughout France there is not a vestige of liberty; for the slightest word or hint they are arrested by the Gend'armes.... Ever since my arrival the scaffolds of France have been streaming with human gore.... The Reign of Terror is now existing every bit as much as in the time of Robespierre, and spies and arrests are equally numerous and frequent.... It is for this that free-born Englishmen have allowed themselves to be gull'd into that war by a set of vile canting hypocrites for their own selfish purposes and to be plunged themselves into unutterable distress!!![33]

---

29 Letter of 28 March 1815, from London.

30 Letter of 29 January 1815, from Paris.

31 Ibid.

32 Letter of 28 March 1815, from London.

33 Letter of 9 August 1816, from Brussels.

He was no fan of the Duke of Wellington, complaining in June 1828 of "a proper bigot Government of Tories with a military bully at their head".[34] Such was his distaste for the governing Tories that Bowes Wright could rarely bring himself to make a favourable comment about British politics in his correspondence. Away from domestic partisanship, his political judgements were sounder.

Planning the expedition to Egypt

In late 1817, before his trip into the Eastern Mediterranean, Bowes Wright was in Venice, hobnobbing with Lord Byron and John Cameron Hobhouse (1786–1869) at the theatre.[35] Thanks to an intervention by Browne with Hobhouse, Byron promised him a letter of introduction to the Albanian 'Alī Pasha (1740–1822), the colourful 'Lion of Joannina' (Ioannina), who had been ruler of Epirus and parts of mainland Greece for the Ottomans since 1787.[36] Bowes Wright would visit him during his meandering return from Cairo, Damascus, and Istanbul in late 1819, only months before 'Alī Pasha was dismissed by Sultan Maḥmūd II.[37] From Egypt, he drew parallels between him and Muḥammad 'Alī as self-made men who, by their exertions, had become largely independent of the Sublime Porte. He later took a strong aversion to 'Alī Pasha of Ioannina once he had visited him and better understood the cruelty and capriciousness of his autocratic rule. Yet he could not help remark that parts of Italy would benefit from 'Alī Pasha's practice of hanging not only road robbers but all members of their families. This had rendered Greece

---

[34] Letter of 9 June 1828, from Paris. Before Waterloo, he had seemed keen on being invited to one of the Duke's grand balls in Paris planned for 18 January 1815, but the event was called off (letter of 29 January 1815, from Paris).

[35] Letter of 7 March 1818, from Rome. "His Lordship generally wore a red cap not unlike a bonnet rouge, but still more like the calotte of a Cardinal. Hobhouse had ornamented himself with a tremendous pair of moustaches, which but for the extreme curvature of his nose, would have rendered it very difficult to recognise him." Hobhouse later became a Whig MP and minister.

[36] Letters of 13 May 1818, from Palermo, and 21 July 1818, from Naples.

[37] In a letter of 31 March 1820, from Vienna, Bowes Wright gives a full description of his adventurous journey from Istanbul through Greece to Trieste, visiting Ioannina on the way.

one of the safest countries in Europe.[38] On the other hand, he noted the "numerous ruined villages" that

> shewed us we were now in the dominions of Ali Pasha. Many of these were the effects of his terrible quarantine; when the plague appears in any part of his territory, he surrounds it with a cordon and no one is allowed to enter or leave it till the malady has ceased; after this the survivors are driven from their homes and the place utterly destroyed.[39]

'Alī Pasha's quarantining methods may have been draconian, but they were effective.

Bowes Wright and his Jesus College friend William Fisher had originally intended to travel to Greece, but were discouraged by the appearance of the plague. Instead they joined forces with Captain Du Cane R.N. and Mr Curteis, who travelled with them from Naples to Malta and had long been set on an expedition to Egypt and Syria.[40] This was not yet a regular trail for foreign travellers, but they were by no means the first to undertake the trip. It had become attractive for the more adventurous British travellers during the Napoleonic wars, when the Grand Tour on the Continent was no longer feasible.[41] The novelty of the destination, new enthusiasm for Egyptology, and keen competition for pharaonic artefacts all sharpened the interest of visitors from Europe. Meanwhile, the trickle of British officers and officials returning from India, no less

---

[38] Letter of 7 March 1818, from Rome.

[39] Letter of 31 March 1820, from Vienna.

[40] Letter of 8 October 1818, from Malta. I have not been able conclusively to identify Du Cane, but he was almost certainly Captain Charles Du Cane RN (1789–1850), one of the Du Canes of Braxted Park, Witham, Essex, who inherited the estate in 1841. He seems to have ended his naval career in 1824–25 as inspecting commander of the Coast Guard. He was a zoologist and expert on crustacea (obituary notice under the rendering Charles Ducane in *Proceedings of the Linnean Society*, 1848–55 ii: 132). Bowes Wright had encountered him in Rome in March 1818 and contemplated a joint local tour (letter of 7 March 1818, from Rome). They journeyed together to Naples, and then to Palermo in May 1818 and seem to have toured Sicily together for over a month (letters of 13 May 1818, from Palermo, and of 21 July 1818, from Naples).

[41] As explained by Legh 1816: v–vi: "A visit to Athens or Constantinople supplied the place of a gay and dissipated winter passed in Paris, Vienna or Petersburgh.... Interviews with the Beys and Pachas of the empire of Mahomet succeeded to the usual presentations at the courts of the Continent."

committed to adventure and to recording their experiences in Egypt, was soon to become a flow.[42] The French official de Forbin said he had often met British officers in Egypt, who were returning from India, as it was an easy transit from Bombay to al-Quṣayr.[43]

Regular and devastating outbreaks of the plague across the region required all travellers to be flexible in their plans, as these could be disrupted with little warning by the plague's capricious progress. It often determined their routes and destinations. As for British hosts in Alexandria and Cairo, regularly bedevilled by disease, homesickness and feelings of isolation, the arrival of these guests brought (old) news of home, the congenial company of their own kind, and the prospect of intellectual and cultural stimulation.

Bowes Wright was filled with confidence about his travel plans on receiving reports in Naples from Lord Belmore (d. 1841), Lady Belmore of Enniskillen and Belmore's brother, Capt. Armar Lowry-Corry R.N. (d. 1855), who had arrived in Naples just before Bowes Wright left in September 1818. In 1817, they had visited Alexandria with a party of twenty, arriving in their own vessel, which started life as the US schooner *James Madison*. Captured by British forces in 1812, it was bought by Belmore, who used it as a privateer and then as a family yacht renamed *Osprey*, until he sold it to the King of Naples after this trip. Belmore may have been spurred to travel by debts at home. Like many well-connected British travellers, he and his party stayed with British Consul General Henry Salt (1780–1827), in the Consular House in Cairo. During this stint, Belmore's personal doctor tended the dying Burckhardt. Belmore and Salt then went up to Luxor in local craft before Belmore went on to Nubia. A sponsor of Giovanni Belzoni (1778–1823), he collected antiquities (and carved his name enthusiastically on monuments) before returning to Cairo in January 1818 and travelling on to Jaffa, Jerusalem, and Damascus. Bowes Wright noted their observations:

> It is perfectly safe travelling in Egypt and very easy, as you are always upon the Nile, in a large commodious boat, some of them

---

[42] As Salt observed in May 1822 to his patron Lord Mountnorris (Halls 1834 ii: 181). He noted the expenses he incurred personally as a result of acting as host to so many visitors from India.

[43] De Forbin 1819: 312.

> being near 70 feet long. Provisions are amazingly cheap, a sheep not costing above a dollar, it is however necessary to go armed and in the Oriental costume and to let your beard grow. From Cairo you cross the desert on Camels and large asses, which are uncommonly swift.[44]

Lowry-Corry gave his naval colleague Du Cane letters of introduction to Muḥammad 'Alī and British consuls in Egypt.

Bowes Wright and his friend William Fisher had travelled together on various previous occasions, for instance visiting the battlefield of Waterloo in early August 1816.[45] Fisher, who was from Liverpool, had graduated from Jesus College, Cambridge in medicine.[46] He appears to have been older and less energetic and adventurous than his friend. He rose later in the morning, did not like dancing and smoked a pipe. Bowes Wright often talked of 'old Fisher' or 'Father Fisher' and once remarked: "Old Fisher prefers quiet to everything".[47] Bowes Wright's silence about his companions on the trip is characteristic of his travelogues. He tends to focus on new encounters or experiences and to omit his travelling companions from his accounts. Hence he leaves us unsure whether Captain Du Cane and Curteis first parted company with Bowes Wright and Fisher in Cairo or later, as Du Cane and Curteis were determined to reach the Second Cataract.[48]

Conscious that their Egyptian venture would be "no trifling tour" and would require proper preparation, Bowes Wright was probably glad of the additional companionship at the outset.[49] He noted before setting out from Malta that "Du Cane has his sextant and other instruments for taking observations and we have a large collection of books of travels in these countries." He reassures Joe: "We are well-armed being also

---

[44] Letter of 8 October 1818, from Malta.

[45] Letter of 9 August 1816, from Brussels.

[46] The will dated 1 March 1850 of William Fisher, Bachelor of Medicine, formerly of Jesus College, of Liverpool, is held at the National Archives. He occasionally refers with Bowes Wright to his "medical authority" (letter from Fisher to Bowes Wright of 5 June 1822, from Paris).

[47] Letter of 14 July 1817, from Florence. In the letter of 13 May 1818, from Palermo, Bowes Wright calls him "that noble veteran".

[48] Letter of 11 April 1819, from Damascus.

[49] Letter of 8 October 1818, from Malta.

provided with fowling pieces, as well for defence as for amusement with the monsters of the Nile." Unconstrained by the Islamic proscriptions of their destination (of which he may have been oblivious), he continues: "We shall carry a large stock of wine, tea, hams and dry provisions."[50] He and his companions were later to use their guns to fire at crocodiles, without making any "impression on their scaly hides".[51]

From Alexandria to Cairo

After Bowes Wright had spent time with the Provincial Grand Master of the Malta Lodge and attended some masonic proceedings, the men left Malta, which Bowes Wright had found insufferably dull after a few days. They departed soon after 8 October, the date of Bowes Wright's last letter from Valletta.[52] Egypt had an active trading relationship with Malta, so passage would not have been hard to arrange. After a tempestuous voyage, their vessel anchored in Aboukir Bay, site of Nelson's famous destruction of the French fleet on 1 August 1798. They disembarked and for two or three days inspected the macabre battlefields of 8 and 13 March 1801, when redcoats had first landed in Egypt ("The strand is yet covered with the bones of men and horses that perished on those memorable days").[53] This was clearly a standard tourist destination for English visitors, as William Bankes, who was up-country with Henry Salt, British consul general 1815–27, during Bowes Wright's visit, toured the same site in 1815.[54]

The party also engaged in quail shooting. This too was a regular pastime for British visitors but, fortunately, Bowes Wright and Fisher avoided the fate of a later British traveller in January/February 1820. He shot a local peasant in the leg by mistake and, on encountering an Albanian with a club who made a threatening gesture, struck him dead

---

[50] Ibid.

[51] Letter of 11 April 1819, from Damascus.

[52] Letter of 8 October 1818, from Malta.

[53] Letter of 18 November 1818, from Cairo (see Appendix A). All subsequent quotations are from this letter, unless otherwise stated.

[54] Usick 2002: 23. Bowes Wright had several conversations with Bankes while in quarantine in the Lazaretto in Trieste in late 1819 (letter of 9 November 1819, from Trieste).

with his musket. The peasants seized him, took him to Cairo, and when the *kiḫyā*, in the pasha's absence, insisted on involving the British consul, the Albanians threatened to ransack the Western quarter and kill any 'Afranj' they found there. So the *kiḫyā* ordered his death and he was beheaded.[55] As the experienced Bowes Wright would have recognised, this was an environment requiring circumspection, not recklessness, on the part of outsiders with little local knowledge.

The party arrived in Alexandria on 21 October, to be confronted by the full-blown unfamiliarity of the East:

> On entering the city our interest was uncommonly excited by the strange and novel aspect of the various objects that presented themselves, the immense camels carrying skins of water on their backs, the Arabs cantering about on swift asses, hideous figures like women with masks upon their faces and muffled up so that only their eyes are visible, every man and boy you meet armed with a prodigious pipe, the dark face of the Ethiopian slave and the grave and pompous deportment of the Turk.

The port town itself did not impress them: "The aspect of its interior is most miserable, and its outskirts are covered to a vast extent with ruins and excavations, the resort of myriads of unclean dogs and vultures and jackalls, which at night fill the air with their howlings."

Bowes Wright and Fisher were fortunate in the support of British officials in Egypt during their visit. They "experienced great hospitality" from Peter Lee, a Levant Company representative, who was also consul in Alexandria from 1814 until his death in 1824.[56] Bowes Wright was relieved that the plague, to which Alexandria was particularly prone and to which it had been badly subjected in the previous two years, had faded from the town, as this meant the visitors could sightsee. They then set off on asses for Rosetta. For Bowes Wright, the town did not live up to its promise ("all is wretched and forlorn"), but the Englishmen were enchanted by their first view of the Nile with the inundation, greater than for twenty years, nearly at its height, and by the river vessels in motion,

---

[55] Al-Jabartī 1958–67 vii: 462.

[56] Wilson 2011: 44. The Levant Company was keeping a close watch on Lee, as it suspected him of fraud (Vlami 2015: 70).

"their immense sails" perfectly resembling shells. In Rosetta, they observed a calvacade containing the harem of the local governor in full *ḥijāb* and mounted on mules, inspected a cache of antiquities from Thebes obtained by Salt, and noted the stores of corn on the Nile's banks. Bowes Wright was quick to grasp the nature of Muḥammad 'Alī's vaunted project to revive Egypt's economy:

> The quantity of corn piled up in heaps at Rosetta along the banks of the Nile is incredible; also of chopped straw for making bricks as in the times of the ancient Israelites; and, as in those days, numerous task-masters may be seen flourishing their whips over the poor Arabs who work as porters in these corn yards. Mahommed Ali Pacha is the sole monopolizer and merchant of the corn trade and indeed of every other trade throughout the land of Egypt. He succeeded to the Pachalic on the expulsion of the [Mamluk] Beys, and like the Pasha of Joannina having raised himself to power by his abilities he has made himself independent of the Porte.

The vice-consul in Rosetta procured a *dgerm* (a large high-pooped Nile boat used for transporting people and goods during the inundation) to take the visitors up to Cairo, a journey that took ten "*mortals jours*". They whiled away the time shooting birds with gratifying results, killing "a great variety of birds unknown in Europe". The party also witnessed a performance at one village of dancing women. In another they attended a wedding, which featured obscene practices Bowes Wright, no prude or stranger to amorous adventures in Europe, found shocking. Finally, once the wind had changed to a gale from the north-west, the travellers were propelled rapidly to within sight of the pyramids, passing through the junction of the Rosetta and Damietta branches of the river and into the remarkable firework display on the evening of Saturday 14 November.

By this point, according to Bowes-Wright, the twenty days of rejoicing at the victory over the Wahhābis were ending, but the exhibitions of naval combat (*naumachiae*) continued.[57] Next morning, Sunday 15 November, they observed

---

[57] As also described by al-Jabartī 1958–67 vii: 445–6, noting that Europeans had created most of the displays.

> the river covered with vessels fitted out like regular men of war and with floating Saracenic castles and temples built upon Dgerms. At noon and again before dark there was a representation of a regular attack upon the castles by the men of war which approached in full sail and under a terrible fire. The effect of such a number of cannon, the rapid movements of the ships on so famous a river as the Nile, the wide extended camp of the cavalry upon its opposite shore, and the number of turbaned spectators on its margin, produced a more pleasing effect than anything I had previously witnessed. At night the ships, castles and town were illuminated, and there was a display of fireworks that would have done honor to Paris or London. I need not add that all this was under the direction of Franks [Europeans], the Pasha being a liberal character, and not caring, if he be served well, whether it be by Mussulman or Christian.

Bowes Wright had already caught wind of the Wahhābis on Malta, where he met the "Great Traveller Rheinard, who has several times crossed the desert from Bagdad to Constantinople, and once defended himself successfully in his caravan against 2,000 Wachabite Arabs".[58] He does not tell us whether he had a substantive or casual social encounter with 'Rheinard', but the latter gave the travellers letters of introduction for Damascus. This individual may have been the shadowy John Lewis Reinaud, a French Catholic and East India Company (EIC) employee. He came from Zante, the Ionian island then ruled by Venice, and was first hired in 1791 to accompany an officer with despatches to Bombay. He then worked with the notoriously cantankerous Samuel Manesty, British Resident in Basra and Kuwait (1784–1810). As a mail courier, he was well travelled in the region. In an uncorroborated account he gave the German traveller Ulrich Seetzen (d. 1811) in April 1805, Reinaud claimed to have been sent by Manesty to al-Dir'iyya to restore good relations between the East India Company and the Sa'ūdis after a Sa'ūdi raid in 1793/94 on Kuwait, where the Company's Basra office was temporarily based.[59] There are several reasons to doubt the accuracy of Reinaud's account of

[58] Letter of 8 October 1818, from Malta.

[59] Seetzen 1805: 237–41. Reproduced in part in Bonacina 2015: 109, n.1. On Reinaud and his alleged visit to al-Dir'iyya, see also Facey 1992: 104–5, 108.

a clash between Company sepoys and the Saʿūdis. He offers no date for his visit, which he maintains occurred in the era of Amir ʿAbd al-ʿAzīz (d. November 1803).[60] That seems to rule him out as the representative Manesty planned to send to al-Dirʿiyya in early 1805 to negotiate the return of British vessels taken by the Qawāsim in the Gulf, two of them owned by Manesty himself.[61]

If Reinaud's visit to al-Dirʿiyya did take place as described, he was the first European to reach the Saʿūdi and Wahhābi capital. If it did not, he was neither the first nor the last traveller in Arabia to invent or embellish experiences there to impress his audience. The tale of a successful defence of a caravan against an improbably high number of Wahhābis suggests 'Rheinard', whoever he was, was given to braggadocio. Listening to such stories in Malta, Bowes Wright can hardly have expected to encounter Wahhābis himself, let alone meet their erstwhile leader in person.

---

60 Seetzen 1805: 240–41.

61 Al-Qasimi, ed. 1995: 35, quoting Bombay Governor Duncan's instructions of 3 March 1805 to Captain Seton, British Resident at Muscat, which do not name Reinaud.

CHAPTER 6

PASHA, IMAM AND WHIG

Imam ʿAbd Allāh arrives in Cairo

Imam ʿAbd Allāh arrived in Cairo on Monday 16 November 1818.[1] Entering by the imposing Bāb al-Naṣr (Victory Gate) on a camel (so that he should be conspicuous for the populace), he had ʿAbd Allāh Baktāsh, port commander (*qubṭān*) at Suez, at his side and was preceded by a troop of light cavalry. The firing of cannon on the citadel, in Būlāq and elsewhere, and fireworks over the Nile, greeted his arrival. Noting the surging crowds on the roads leading to the busy port area of Būlāq, al-Jabartī wrote of the displays and festivities in a tone of wonder echoing that of Bowes Wright: "This was one of the strangest performances for which there had been no precedent in Egypt, nor anything like it." The crowds dispersed, and Muḥammad ʿAlī made his way by boat to his Shubrā Palace.[2]

The original plan had been for the Saʿūdi imam to go straight to Shubrā that day but, as Bowes Wright recorded, for some reason the meeting was postponed until the following afternoon. ʿAbd Allāh was therefore escorted to the house of Ismāʿīl Pasha in Būlāq, where he was lodged. He was brought to the Shubrā Palace for a meeting with Muḥammad ʿAlī next day, Tuesday 17 November. The pasha had been preparing to leave Cairo and on the day of the imam's arrival was due to hold court at

---

[1] According to al-Jabartī 1958–67 vii: 446. Inaccurately, Mengin gives his arrival date in Cairo as 17 November and says he went straight to Shubrā to meet the pasha (1823 ii: 139–40).

[2] Al-Jabartī 1958–67 vii: 446.

Shubrā before departure. Bowes Wright, with his strong political interests, and Fisher were keen to be presented to him. Samuel Briggs (1767–1853 or *ca.* 1776–1868), whom the former described as the British consul, while noting his business partnership with the pasha in relation to corn exports, undertook to arrange this.

British official representation and commercial business

Briggs was a merchant and banker of long standing in Alexandria who had previously acted as pro-consul and representative of the Levant Company in Alexandria 1803–10, tasked with obtaining wheat for British forces. He then set up his own firm in Alexandria in 1804, and another one in London in 1811.[3] Until about 1813, grain exports from Alexandria were vital for British interests in Malta, Sicily, and Spain.[4] Briggs was involved with the pasha in the grain trade (as Bowes Wright notes) and then in the export of Egyptian cotton to the Lancashire mills, a business he pioneered. He also traded with India in partnership with the pasha from 1816.[5] As Ottoman *wālī*, Muḥammad ʿAlī was required to accept the official representatives of outside powers, yet never acquired the right from the Ottomans to appoint his own representatives to foreign capitals. He therefore aimed to give himself leverage through joint business ventures with British merchants, who might help shape British policy in favour of his own objectives.[6] For many years Briggs proved an effective agent of influence for him.

Gradually in this period, it became prescribed as part of British official arrangements overseas that traders should not act as officials, nor should officials conduct commercial affairs on their own account. Because of the patent risks of corruption, conflicts of interest, and distortion of foreign policy, such practices had been prohibited in the Indian administration as long ago as the 1760s. The ban was finally extended to the Bombay presidency, which oversaw British interests in the Gulf, in 1804, then to

---

3 Anon. 1826: 424. According to the court deposition in *Buckingham v. Bankes*, up until 1826 Briggs lived in Egypt in four spells, 1802–7, 1809–10, 1816–17 and 1818–19 (ibid.).

4 Letter of Missett to Cooke of 14 October 1813 (FO 24/4) in Burdett 2013 i: 346–7.

5 De Forbin 1819: 307. The later relationship between Briggs and the pasha is explored in Rodkey 1933.

6 Rodkey 1933: 325.

Muscat in 1805, and to Būshahr in 1822. British representatives in the Gulf had previously been exempted from the rule on the basis that they held no administrative or executive powers.[7]

Change was under way too in Egypt, where there had been a longstanding arrangement involving both the Levant Company and the Foreign Office in the selection of representatives, although from 1804 the Crown made the appointments and paid for the consul general.[8] The Levant Company was dissolved in 1825 and the British government then assumed exclusive responsibility for appointing consuls in the Levant, who were brigaded into the Consular Service formed by Foreign Secretary George Canning (d. 1827) in that year. Until then, and indeed for some years thereafter, British representatives continued to pursue commercial interests. Peter Lee, who looked after Bowes Wright in Alexandria as the Levant Company's vice-consul in that city, was a member of Briggs's firm.[9] Robert Thurburn (1784–1860), a partner of Briggs, who had managed his Alexandria office and accommodated Consul General Salt when he took over Lee's duties in Alexandria as well as performing his own in Cairo, became consul in Cairo 1833–38, apparently at the instigation of the pasha.[10] A friend of Salt noted that his efforts in the cause of literature and research did much to remove "the impression entertained by foreigners, that our official agents abroad are apt to make their public station entirely 'subservient to their private interest'".[11]

When Bowes Wright gave Briggs the title of 'consul', this may have been purely honorific, since by 1818 he had long since ceased to serve the Crown officially. Equally, Briggs, as someone in regular contact with the pasha, may have agreed formally or informally to stand in for the absent Salt, who had such a high opinion of Briggs that he made him one of his daughter's two trustees under his will.[12] In 1821, Salt told his patron

[7] Lorimer 1915 i (Pt 1A): 162, 212–13.

[8] Bosworth 1974: 78–9.

[9] Rodkey 1933: 328.

[10] Ibid. : 330.

[11] Halls 1834 ii: 293.

[12] Ibid. ii: 278. In a letter of introduction to Halls of 7 May 1819, Salt described his friend Briggs as long "at the head of the first mercantile establishment in Egypt. He is a gentleman of sound principles and highly liberal feelings." (ibid. ii: 111). In another similar letter of 4 May to William Hamilton, he emphasized Briggs's knowledge of

Lord Mountnorris (formerly Viscount Valentia, a Freemason) that Briggs was the only person to whom he could entrust the consulate.[13] Briggs also kept Salt afloat financially, as by December 1816 the latter's salary was seriously in arrears.[14] The collection and sale of antiquities, which Salt's patron Sir Joseph Banks, President of both the Royal Society and the African Association and a trustee of the British Museum (as well as a Freemason), had encouraged him to undertake, would later give Salt greater financial security.

In October 1818, Salt was in the south of the country in or near Thebes, engaged with his increasingly disaffected assistant Giovanni Belzoni in their regular and highly lucrative pursuit of ancient Egyptian artefacts in sharp competition with the French.[15] Near Rosetta Bowes Wright, who was later to become a friend of Belzoni,[16] had examined one of his stashes of antiquities from Thebes awaiting collection and shipment to London. Salt did not return to Cairo until March 1819, when he was compelled to do so by both business and severe sickness.[17] French Consul Drovetti was also around Thebes, pursuing an increasingly acrimonious rivalry with Salt and Belzoni that the French recognised was a losing battle against "the new masters of Egypt".[18] Relations between the British and French missions were poor.

In May 1819, Salt, still affected by the loss of Burckhardt, sadly told a London friend that the generality of his acquaintance were enemies rather than friends. He expressed his sense of isolation in an alien environment: "Neither morning nor evening is ever ushered in with the glad countenance of a friend, but all is outward courtesy, too generally

---

both Egypt and Salt's affairs. Briggs was involved to a degree in assisting with the transportation of antiquities. One piece he hand-delivered was a Ptolemaic gold plate that was a present from the pasha to Sir William Sidney Smith, who had helped defend Acre from Napoleon in 1799 (ibid. ii: 114).

[13] Ibid. ii: 180. See also ibid. ii: 218.

[14] Bosworth 1974: 80.

[15] Ironically, Salt was so discouraged by his experience with the British Museum in relation to its purchase of his first collection that he sold the second one directly to the French government through Champollion.

[16] He visited Belzoni's mother in Padua soon after Belzoni's death (fragment of a letter, presumably to Joseph Lamb, of *ca.* August 1825, from Italy).

[17] Halls 1834 ii: 124.

[18] De Forbin 1819: 266–7, 316.

and too justly mingled with contempt for one's company." For him, one of the virtues of plague-related quarantine, then in force, was that it kept enemies at bay.[19] Among his guests and friends enduring this quarantine was the Anglican Rev. William Jowett (1787–1855), Fellow of St John's, Cambridge, 1811–16, who in 1813 had become a missionary based in Malta.[20] Most of the Cambridge *alumni* who travelled to Egypt at this time were from just three colleges: Jesus, St John's and Trinity.

Previous British experiences of the pasha and the imam

Bowes Wright offers a picture of the open-minded, modernising pasha having a relatively close link with the British at this time, while the imam is a 'rebel'. There is no awareness in his correspondence of the curious paradox presented by these two leaders' previous interactions with the British. He might naturally have assumed that, since the Wahhābis regarded Christians as further along the spectrum of unbelief even than other Muslims against whom they waged jihad, the Saʿūdis would have been actively hostile to the British presence in the Gulf. Instead, they pursued an entirely pragmatic policy towards the British authorities in India. They would have preferred the British not to be in the Gulf at all, but were realists and, recognising their own maritime weakness, tolerated their presence. By contrast, Muḥammad ʿAlī's government had been involved in a bloody and religiously tinged war with British forces only ten years before, fought over ground covered by Bowes Wright and his companions on their journey to Cairo. Leading Egyptian notables had called this conflict jihad against unbelievers (*kuffār*), labelling the British the enemies of Islam.[21]

The pointless British campaign in the Nile Delta in 1807, allegedly the brainchild of Consul-General Missett, was misconceived and disastrously mismanaged. The small force of 6,000 men occupied Alexandria in March that year, but failed to take Rosetta and suffered one bloody setback after another, until, stricken with casualties and disease, it evacuated Alexandria

[19] Letter to Mary Halls of 22 May 1819, in Halls 1834 ii: 127.

[20] Ibid. ii: 124.

[21] Al-Jabartī 1958–67 vi: 355–61. Whereas al-Jabartī claims Muḥammad ʿAlī took fright at the invasion, al-Rajabī portrays him as playing a courageous role in the victory (1997: 22 [comment by Crecelius, ed.]).

under a truce with Muḥammad ʿAlī in September.[22] In the interval, some of the British captives were decapitated. About 340 British heads were paraded in Cairo and then put up on display in al-Azbakiyya, while 466 prisoners, including twenty officials, were lodged in the citadel, where they were well treated, thanks largely to French intervention on their behalf.[23] French Consul Drovetti even received a personal letter of thanks from the British commander ("the British Nation will ever feel indebted to you").[24] The heads were eventually buried, while the ears were cut off, tanned and sent on to Istanbul, via Syria, in a box accompanied by two of the captured British army officers.[25]

This grim episode took place at roughly the time of the Saʿūdi appropriation of the Prophet's treasures and a mere eleven years before Bowes Wright's visit. Oddly, since he traversed the same country and staged in Rosetta, he does not mention this gory struggle, whereas he and Fisher record their inspection of the battlefields of March 1801. Even if a discreet veil had been drawn over the conflict in bilateral contacts, the expulsion of the invaders represented a significant military achievement by the Albanian soldiers in Egypt, of which the later British-led victory over the French at Waterloo made the pasha even more proud.[26] It did not dispel his anxieties about British territorial ambitions. He seems to have expected yet another British descent on Egypt in 1815, directly after Waterloo.[27]

By contrast, the British and the Saʿūdis had both been careful to avoid conflict with each other in the Gulf, even when the expansion of Saʿūdi rule and influence along the littoral brought them up against each other and led to a clash of interests, especially in respect of Muscat. The Saʿūdi line, set by Imam Saʿūd and maintained by Imam ʿAbd Allāh, was grounded in political and military expediency, not religious creed or ideology. They recognised that it was not in their interests to confront the

---

[22] The geopolitical context and campaign are well outlined in Pocock 2005: 75–88.

[23] Al-Jabartī 1958–67 vi: 369–70.

[24] Ridley (n.d.): 47, quoting General Fraser's letter of 7 May 1807.

[25] Al-Jabartī 1958–67 vi: 373–4. The officers, apparently despatched by the pasha at the instigation of Drovetti, were the Swiss Major Charles Vogelsang and Lieutenant John Love (Ridley [n.d.]: 47–8).

[26] De Forbin 1819: 304–5. See also al-Jabartī 1958–67 vi: 370.

[27] Burckhardt 1831 ii: 354–5.

premier naval and trading power in the region, while the British were determined to avoid a military entanglement with Arabia's major land power. After circling each other warily, the two sides arrived from 1810 at a workable *modus vivendi* that amounted to a non-hostility pact. Although in exchanges this was often expressed, with diplomatic nicety, as 'amity', it never developed into a formal treaty of friendship, although Imam Saʿūd applied unsuccessfully to the British for one in August 1813 and early 1814. The British in India were unenthusiastic, probably because they did not wish to upset the Ottomans, but also as the prevailing bilateral accommodation was being increasingly tested by the maritime violence of the Qawāsim of Rās al-Khayma and associated ports in the lower Gulf. That persisted until 1819.

The Qawāsim adhered to Wahhābism and often acted as Saʿūdi surrogates in seizing the shipping of their many common enemies. For them this was jihad; for the British, it was 'piracy', especially when the vessels attacked and plundered, not just in the Gulf, but from 1806 off the coast of India, belonged to the East India Company, or carried British colours or passes. The British assured Imam Saʿūd in mid-1810 that:

> the British Government does not concern itself with the hostilities carried on by him [Saʿūd] against the Members of the Mussulman faith, on account of their alleged deviation from the ordinances of the Koran, and that its power will alone be directed against those who exercising the detestible profession of Piracy are the common enemies of all nations.[28]

This statement shows the extent to which the two powers were culturally at cross-purposes and politically at odds. What the British saw as an unequivocal declaration of intent to suppress piracy appeared to the Saʿūdis *carte blanche* for them to operate against their enemies at sea. Yet, however much the two powers talked past each other, they never came directly to blows.

The British attacked Rās al-Khayma in 1809 to punish and deter the Qawāsim, but the latter swiftly resumed and intensified their violence

---

[28] Letter of Chief Secretary Edmonstone, Calcutta to Chief Secretary Warden, Bombay of 7 July 1810 in IOR F/4/3441/7963: 303–5 at 304; letter of Governor Duncan of Bombay to Imam Saʿūd of 9 August 1810, quoted by J.A. Saldana, *Persian Gulf Gazetteer*, p. 7, para 25 in Burdett 2013 i: 72.

under more direct Sa'ūdi control of the port. Governors-general in India refused to risk a conflict with al-Dir'iyya by retaliating with force against the Qawāsim and other Sa'ūdi surrogates, despite growing British anger and frustration. These led to heavy British pressure on the Qawāsim for the restitution of, or compensation for, plundered vessels and goods belonging to British subjects in India. Sa'ūdi–British bilateral exchanges became tense in early 1817, eighteen months before the fall of al-Dir'iyya, after British ships staged a singularly ineffective demonstration of firepower off Rās al-Khayma in late 1816. This episode angered Imam 'Abd Allāh, who had been conducting intermittent correspondence with the British representative in the Gulf, Būshahr-based Resident William Bruce, since 1814.[29] Claiming the Qawāsim as his subjects, he launched a barrage of complaints in an aggrieved and threatening tone.[30] Imam 'Abd Allāh pronounced:

> If then your late proceedings were effected with a view to rousing us to war, and of destroying the bonds of alliance, God's will be done. Your dependence, however, on us and the policy of preserving unbroken the relations of amity are on your side more imperiously necessary than on ours.[31]

This misread both the situation and the balance of power and advantage. Sa'ūdi influence on the coast was already greatly diminished; Imam 'Abd Allāh himself was subject to heavy military pressure from Ibrāhīm Pasha; and a military confrontation with the British would only have created another front for the beleaguered leader. The British had only to wait for the Āl Sa'ūd's downfall to bombard Rās al-Khayma in late 1819 and enforce maritime peace in the Gulf. In mid-1819, they sent an unsuccessful mission into Arabia to seek Ibrāhīm Pasha's commitment

---

[29] The first occasion was in October 1814 in relation to an alleged attack by the Qawāsim on a British ship (translated text of a letter to Resident Bruce, Būshahr, attached to Bruce's letter to Governor Sir Evan Nepean of Bombay of 11 October 1814 in IOR/R/15/1/14: 242–3).

[30] Translated texts in IOR/R/15/1/19 of three undated letters from Imam 'Abd Allāh to Bruce, the first probably of February 1817: 40–41 (the text has been damaged and some of it is missing), the second received 11 April 1817: 47–48, and the third of late April 1817: 53–54.

[31] Translated text of undated letter from Imam 'Abd Allāh to Bruce received at Būshahr 11 April 1817 in IOR/R/15/1/19: 48.

to assault Rās al-Khayma by land, while they attacked from the sea. Ibrāhīm was interested to be in contact with the British authorities in India, but events had overtaken the British proposal and the pashas did not appear much impressed by the initiative.[32] They would have recalled that the British had remained studiedly neutral throughout the Arabian war and declined a request from Muḥammad ʿAlī for maritime assistance.

The English travellers visit Shubrā Palace

That the pasha should have been so ready to see British visitors to Cairo, who held no official position and exercised no discernible political influence in London, may seem curious, but, as an Ottoman governor, he was not in a position to post representatives to third countries. He therefore used meetings with Western visitors to project his image in European capitals, in the expectation that they would write at least some of these sessions up for Western readerships with an interest in the east.[33] This was a successful approach, for in Western travel accounts of the period his is a constant, towering, presence. As a result, many more influential figures in European cities became familiar with his achievements and activities than if he had made himself accessible only to the few Western officials in Cairo, who reported into the chancelleries of Europe.

The pasha's desire to raise his international profile, as much as personal vanity, also lay behind his readiness to have his portrait drawn or painted by Western artists, such as le Comte de Forbin (March 1818),[34] Auguste Couder (1840), Sir David Wilkie (1841), and Thomas Brigstocke (1847–48). His interest in seeing Europeans, and extending them his protection, including when engaged in acquisitive archaeological activities,[35] encouraged Western visitors, and ultimately helped to establish the modern tourism industry in Egypt.

At 7 a.m. on Monday 16 November 1818, Briggs, Bowes Wright, and Fisher, all in European dress, as was the visitors' practice in Egypt, set

---

[32] Sadleir 1866: 81–7.

[33] Fahmy 2002: 3.

[34] De Forbin 1819: 224 (ibid.: 304: "When intimacy had been established between us, Mohamed Aly allowed me to draw his portrait").

[35] Salt noted the "liberality" of Muḥammad ʿAlī, "who … exerted himself to facilitate the researches carried on by Europeans connected with science" (Halls 1834 ii: 102–3).

off from the Consular House in al-Azbakiyya, leased from Muḥammad 'Alī, for the pasha's palace at Shubrā three miles away mounted on Arabian horses belonging to the consulate.[36] We do not know if they were accompanied by Captain Du Cane or Curteis, or indeed any other British visitors.[37] Their destination was Muḥammad 'Alī's retreat from the governor's traditional residence in the citadel and from his own house in al-Azbakiyya, a low-lying green part of Cairo, which featured a lake for three months a year and served as a garden for the remainder. In subsequent decades, al-Azbakiyya became the centre of an increasingly intrusive Western community, but at the time it was in a badly damaged state, thanks to a bombardment by French forces that had turned the quarter into "un monceau de ruines" (a heap of ruins).[38]

Shubrā Palace was set in a rural area of northern Cairo, covered 150 acres, and featured well-cultivated gardens, irrigated by machine-driven waterwheels installed in a tower built in 1811. The pasha was determined to put distance between himself and the mêlée of everyday Cairo, even if the citadel remained his refuge in times of trouble (as in 1815) and the place where his deputy (*kiḥyā*) continued to perform his duties when the pasha was away.[39] From early 1809, the pasha had a palace constructed, together with various smaller pavilions, based on Istanbul styles, in grounds sloping gently down to the waters of the Nile.[40] It was later to consist of two major buildings, the Fisqiyya and the Gabalāya, which, in their eclectic mix of European, Arab, and Ottoman styles, represented a visual statement of the pasha's break with the past and his autonomy of Istanbul. He moved into the palace in 1810 and extended it in 1812.

---

[36] The Consular House was in Darb al-Barābira, according to al-Jabartī, who visited it in the previous year in the company of Burckhardt (1958–67 vii: 419).

[37] For instance, Bowes Wright later mentions having met Captain Foskett in Egypt (letter of 6 November 1819, from Trieste). He was presumably Henry Foskett, formerly of the 15th Light Dragoons, whose participation in a duel in 1806 became a *cause célèbre* in 1810–11.

[38] De Forbin 1819: 209.

[39] As with the call by the new French Consul General Joseph Roussel and de Forbin in late December 1817/early January 1818 (ibid.: 210–11).

[40] Al-Jabartī 1958–67 vii: 46. In recording the events of the month in which construction started, the historian underlines the distressed state of the people, thanks to oppressive government (ibid.).

That the pasha was about to have the palace recast (and electric lighting installed) in 1821, not long after his meeting with Imam ʿAbd Allāh, suggests he was not content with the first version that Bowes Wright and Fisher saw. The designer for the palace's development was the French engineer and architect Pascal Coste (1787–1879), who had been in Cairo since 1 November 1817.[41] He received the instruction in 1821: "Le pacha voulait en faire un petit Versailles, avec bosquets, labyrinthe, hippodrome, grande pièce d'eau entourée de galeries, avec quatre pavillons divan ; d'une [*sic* ; une] chapelle-mosquée et de grandes allées bordées d'arbres."[42] In the end, his drawings were amended by Turkish and Armenian architects, to his annoyance, but he did design the gardens.[43] In all, the palace projected the pasha's capacity to establish order and to impress.[44]

The visitors, accompanied by Briggs, rode along what would soon become Shubrā Avenue, "the fashionable promenade of Cairo".[45] This would subsequently be "shaded with magnificent sycamore and acacia trees, that interlace their branches over the wide road, forming a green bower the whole way".[46] Bowes Wright observed that they were "amidst an immense number of Mamalukes and Cavaliers splendidly dressed and mounted upon horses, asses and dromedaries". The embassy escort doubtless provided protection in the crush from the rough encounters that foreigners could experience in Egypt.[47] On arrival, they walked through the harem portion of the palace (*al-ḥarāmlik*) in the absence of the females. Bowes Wright found some of the apartments "handsome and not badly painted in Arabesque". Although he had been told to expect "a

---

41 A valuable chronology for Coste's two stints in Egypt is at Zivie 1998: 174.

42 Coste 1998: 40: "The pasha wanted a little Versailles, with groves, a labyrinth, a hippodrome, a large ornamental lake surrounded by galleries, with four pavilions, a chapel-mosque and great avenues flanked by trees."

43 Ashmouni and Bartsch 2014: 63.

44 Ibid.: 64.

45 Reynolds-Ball 1899: 161.

46 Fairholt 1862: 56–7. The trees appear to have been planted in the 1820s (ibid.: 57).

47 In 1815 Belzoni, Salt's future assistant in acquiring artefacts, received a blow from a passing soldier in Cairo that removed flesh from his leg and put him out of action for a month. This was during the mutiny in Cairo. Muḥammad ʿAlī, used to disaffected or undisciplined soldiery, commented coolly: "Such accidents could not be avoided where there were troops" (Belzoni 1820: 7–8, quotation at 8). De Forbin was attacked by a drunken Albanian soldier in Damietta in late 1817 (1819: 199–200).

grand Court to be held previous to [the pasha's] departure", he does not mention it.

Muḥammad ʿAlī welcomes the visitors

Bowes Wright and the others were summoned to the pasha. According to Bowes Wright's description, he was seated on the divan in one corner of the room, smoking a hookah more than fifteen feet long.[48] Seated near him was the pasha's deputy, variously entitled *kiḥyā bey*, *katkhudā bey*, or *qā'immaqām*. This was Muḥammad Bey Lāẓ, a close and trusted associate, whose family came from near Trabzon on the Black Sea, and whom Muḥammad ʿAlī was soon abruptly to dismiss.[49] All the other courtiers stood. After the visitors had been presented, they joined the pasha on the divan and sat near him while coffee was brought.

The pasha does not seem to have stage-managed the scene as carefully as he did in later years with foreign callers to the refashioned palace. Bowes Wright does not mention the features that impressed many visitors so forcibly, and which they recorded with striking consistency: the busy antechamber, the pasha sitting shrouded in shadow, the piercing gaze.[50] Since Bowes Wright was both observant and ready, even eager, to be impressed, his account suggests the pasha had not yet honed his technique for imprinting his remarkable personality on visitors, or adopted the theatricality that became his hallmark with foreign callers.

Grasping the opportunity presented by the British visitors, Muḥammad ʿAlī informed them of the arrival of Imam ʿAbd Allāh that very day and the deferral of his meeting with him to the following day. This mention carried an implicit invitation to the Englishmen to attend the planned encounter. The pasha had an interest in the British witnessing and reporting the crowning moment of his personal triumph over the Wahhābis, which represented a considerable political and military achievement. He wanted to exploit the occasion to raise his international standing, and to show that

---

[48] De Forbin observed that in Alexandria the pasha smoked a pipe covered in precious stones (1819: 301). Bankes described the handle of the pipe the pasha was smoking in the citadel in 1815 as covered in diamonds (Usick 2002: 25).

[49] Al-Jabartī 1958–67 vii: 425; Mengin 1823 ii: 147–8. The pasha replaced him in mid-February 1819 (al-Jabartī 1958–67 vii: 452).

[50] Fahmy 2002: 3–8.

he had come of age as a regional force in his own right, and was no longer merely an Ottoman instrument. He would have been keen to have the event reported back to London.

Personal impressions of Muḥammad ʿAlī and his court

Already by 1818, the pasha's achievements had made him a figure of interest and curiosity for Westerners. Bowes Wright was impressed by the pasha's "fine intelligent countenance". He guessed his age to be fifty-five (he was forty-eight). He noted that from time to time he made a peculiar noise with his throat that the visitors were told resulted from a severe cold, but which sounded to Bowes Wright "more like the formidable and lengthened 'Aha' of our Harry 8th [English King Henry VIII]". De Forbin, who had had numerous long meetings with the pasha in Alexandria earlier in the year, described his conversation as punctuated by a kind of convulsive hiccough ("une sorte de hoquet convulsif"), which he was told was the result of a violent poison.[51]

Significantly for one with a Whig's progressive convictions and hatred for tyranny, Bowes Wright took a lenient view of the pasha's treacherous massacre of the mamlūks in 1811 and offers a favourable view of him:

> Except the murder of the Beys, which was perhaps a matter of self-defence, I have heard him charged with no other cruelties; he has rendered his territories the safest in the East to travel in; and though he monopolises the trade of the country, he has increased its natural production in a wonderful degree. He is a most anxious encourager of arts and manufacture in Egypt, and for their better cultivation has founded a magnificent establishment in Cairo. He has extended his dominion to the cataracts on one side and over the desert to the Indian Ocean on the other having re-conquered Mecca and Medina from the Wachabites.

Some Western callers in future years were to be even more enthusiastic; others took a less forgiving view. Two Royal Navy captains, who visited Cairo the previous year but did not meet the pasha, commented succinctly:

---

[51] 1819: 302.

"Could such an atrocious crime as the murder of the mamelukes be overlooked, he might be considered as a great man."[52]

It is illuminating to compare Bowes Wright's favourable picture and assessment of Muḥammad ʿAlī with his view of ʿAlī Pasha of Ioannina, on whom he called in late 1819, and who asked him about his travels in Egypt and about Muḥammad ʿAlī, who was originally from the Balkans. During that conversation, the translator spoke Romaic to ʿAlī Pasha and Italian to Bowes Wright. Probably because he had more opportunity to study ʿAlī Pasha in his den and afterwards more time to write at length from Vienna, Bowes Wright's physical description of the "hoary ruffian" ʿAlī Pasha is more detailed than that of Muḥammad ʿAlī. He concludes: "Notwithstanding the civilities I received from Ali Pasha, truth compells me to declare that from all the dreadful things I heard of him, I consider him one of the cruellest tyrants and bloodiest villains, according to his capacity, that ever ruled over a wretched people."

Although he was alarmed at one point in Meteora, while on a narrow hill path, to be tapped on the shoulder by "the Eunuch-maker of Ali Pasha, a man of a monstrous and Caliban-like appearance", he was personally well treated in ʿAlī Pasha's domains. Yet, after offering examples of the pasha's debauchery, callous brutality and oppression, he protests:

> Notwithstanding all these horrid doings, this monster still continues to live and reign, and England, so hypocritically squeamish about treating with Napoleon not only continues to treat with him, but has delivered the Christian town of Parga into his hands; and every one of its inhabitants has been driven into exile and ruin. Of all the hateful and inconsistent feats of my Lord Castlereagh, this is to me the most inexplicable.

He earlier referred sarcastically to this episode as Foreign Secretary Castlereagh's (d. 1822) "brilliant achievement".[53] Yet some among Bowes Wright's British acquaintances counted ʿAlī Pasha a friend.[54]

---

[52] Irby and Mangles 1845: 50. Bowes Wright expected to meet Charles Irby (d. 1845) and James Mangles (d. 1867) in Trieste in late 1820 (letter of 6 November 1820, from Trieste).

[53] The quotations in this paragraph all come from Bowes Wright's extended letter of 31 March 1820, from Vienna.

[54] Letter of William Jones to Bowes Wright of 5 April 1822, from Naples.

Bowes Wright's Whiggish prejudices are on full display here, not only in the condemnation of Tory Lord Castlereagh, a particular hate figure for the Whigs, but in his caustic comment about British policy towards Napoleon. Whig sympathy for Napoleon was notorious and had recently been demonstrated by effusive concern for his welfare after his defeat at Waterloo.[55] Yet Napoleon had himself sometimes displayed vicious bloodthirstiness, never more so than outside Jaffa in 1799, when French invading troops under his command, and on his explicit written orders, systematically massacred about three thousand of Governor of Acre Aḥmad Pasha al-Jazzār's troops in the dunes.[56] The Ottoman soldiery took this to justify their decapitation of French prisoners during the campaign to reoccupy Egypt in 1801, despite the British general's remonstrations, "such enormities being so incredibly atrocious".[57]

Muḥammad 'Alī, who was to send his first educational mission to Paris in 1826, took a sanguine view of the French occupation of Egypt and was even complimentary about the French forces.[58] He had great respect both for Napoleon and for France as the premier military power on land. He cultivated close relations with the French and saw various Frenchmen, especially Drovetti, regularly and showed them considerable kindness.[59] Ibrāhīm Pasha was accompanied to the Hijaz by two Bonapartist officers in 1816.[60] One of them, Joseph Vaissière, a former engineers officer, had a positive influence on Ibrāhīm's campaign strategy after a major setback, and the pasha spoke eloquently to de Forbin of his contribution.[61] The pasha also relied on a diminishing band of French soldiers who had stayed

---

[55] Mitchell 2007: 88–91.

[56] Roberts 2014: 189–91. Philipp comments: "Napoleon probably had more people killed there in one day than Aḥmad Pasha al-Jazzār ['the Butcher', a byword in cruelty] killed in a lifetime" (2001: 57). De Forbin's odd excuse is that, having taken the town, the French had massacred a great number of Christians in the Christian quarter, thinking they were Muslims (1819: 134, n.1). Fittingly, the French soldiers caught the plague off Jaffa's inhabitants. When Napoleon retreated from Jaffa, he is reputed to have poisoned thirty-five of his own men, who were sick in hospital, to prevent them falling into Ottoman hands (Irby and Mangles 1845: 58).

[57] Wilson 1803: 63–4 (quotation at 64).

[58] De Forbin 1819: 305.

[59] Ibid.: 225–6.

[60] Burckhardt 1831 ii: 356–7.

[61] De Forbin 1819: 287; Ridley n.d.: 78. See also Mengin 1823 ii: 137.

behind after the French occupation to become Muslims and mamlūks. By 1818, the original total of eight hundred had been whittled down by conflict and plague to a mere eighty. They sometimes served as the pasha's bodyguard, although they complained of being neglected and poorly paid.[62] His respect and affection for the French, which was matched by a French belief in a special bilateral affinity with Egypt, did not stop the pasha conveying puzzlement to a British visitor as to why the British had not cut off Napoleon's head after his defeat at Waterloo.[63]

Bowes Wright condemned 'Alī Pasha of Ioannina, while lauding Muḥammad 'Alī and excusing his slaughter of the mamlūks, an action described by de Forbin as the most remarkable piece of treachery ("la plus insigne perfidie").[64] In the Frenchman's view, the pasha was violent and brooked no contradiction, but he was not bloodthirsty ("sanguinaire").[65] Perhaps, if questioned on this, Bowes Wright would have responded that, unlike 'Alī Pasha's capricious brutality, Muḥammad 'Alī's violence was considered or calculated, not gratuitous or pursued for its own sake. But the apparent double standard may be better explained by traditional Whiggish approbation for rulers viewed as reformers and modernisers, however autocratic and oppressive they were to their own subjects. Unlike the traditionalist 'Alī Pasha, Muḥammad 'Alī was a reformer and moderniser, if ruthless in pursuit of 'progress'. In the end, both men rebelled against Sultan Maḥmūd, 'Alī Pasha with markedly less success than Muḥammad 'Alī. He was shot while resisting Ottoman forces in Ioannina in 1822 and then decapitated. His head was sent to the Sublime Porte to be placed on display.

Bowes Wright had little occasion or opportunity to appreciate the downsides of Muḥammad 'Alī's regime. He noted soon after arrival: "The relation of tyrant and slave is legibly written on the faces of one or other of all the Orientals I have seen." Yet he arrived in Cairo at a time of

---

[62] De Forbin 1819: 211. The British equivalents were the Scotsman Thomas Keith (Ibrāhīm Āghā) and the well-known dragoman Osman, who, as William Thompson and a British soldier, had been captured and enslaved at Rosetta in 1807, only to be freed by the pasha in 1815. Bowes Wright makes no mention of him. By a curious symmetry, Napoleon employed mamlūks as his personal bodyguards in Paris.

[63] Usick 2002: 25.

[64] De Forbin 1819: 222.

[65] Ibid.: 224.

festivities and celebration and did not have the same chance as de Forbin to discern how downtrodden most Cairenes were ("chacun dans ce pays desire une révolution"[66]), subject to a government "purement militaire, tout dépend de la volunté du chef".[67] Unlike de Forbin, the Englishman did not observe the negative impact of the pasha's grip on the economy exercised through the monopolies in major trades that he had established a few years before.[68] Bowes Wright too knew little of the gruesome realities of the Arabian war, to the savagery of which the pasha had contributed personally. Nor, as a Whig uninterested in religion, could he see that the Wahhābis were radical religious reformers, while in this arena Muḥammad ʻAlī was content to represent the forces of traditionalism.

Ismāʻīl Pasha, the imam's host

The English visitors, who would have spoken English or French for the interpreter to translate into Ottoman Turkish, were also presented to the *silaḥdār*, the master-at-arms or master-general of the ordnance, who dealt with property matters, the recently appointed Sulaymān Āghā.[69] They met too another celebrated Egyptian notable, Shaykh Shadīd, the powerful chief of the al-Ḥuwayṭāt tribal confederacy. This had sided from the outset with the invading Ottoman forces because the Saʻūdi block on the Egyptian hajj had deprived it of its main revenue source.[70] Shaykh Shadīd had won a small victory against the future Imam ʻAbd Allāh and ʻUthmān al-Muḍāīfī in a clash outside Yanbuʻ in the first days of the campaign.[71] Famously, as Bowes Wright noted, he had endorsed and commended the conduct of his wife in saving the life of his mortal enemy, mamlūk leader Alfī Bey (d. 1807), by giving him hospitality. Finally, they encountered Ismāʻīl Pasha, the pasha's son, now in his early twenties, whom the visitors might have expected to be attending his Wahhābi captive in Būlāq.

---

[66] Ibid.: 210.

[67] Ibid.: 309.

[68] See ibid. De Forbin described the monopolies as hateful.

[69] Al-Jabartī 1958–67 vii: 426.

[70] Marsot 1984: 200. He is mentioned in Mengin's list of tribes and tribal chiefs (1823 ii: 307).

[71] Al-Jabartī 1958–67 vii: 146.

In 1813, Ismāʿīl had been privileged to convey to Istanbul the keys to the Holy Cities on their recapture, which were then placed in the Holy Relics Room in the Topkapi Palace with much celebration.[72] This was the point at which the sultan, with his legitimacy as caliph restored, assumed the title '*ghāzī*' (holy warrior). In late June, a decree arrived in Cairo from the Sublime Porte instructing those delivering the Friday sermons in the mosques to include in the regular prayer for the sultan after his name the phrase '*al-mughāzī khādim al-ḥaramayn al-sharīfayn*' (holy warrior and custodian of the two Holy Places). This was based on a *fatwā* labelling the Wahhābis unbelievers (*kuffār*) for their own excommunication (*takfīr*) of other Muslims and rebellion against the sultan, while those dying in the struggle against them qualified as martyrs (*shuhadā'*). The reading of this decree triggered the firing of cannon from the citadel and in Būlāq and al-Gīza.[73]

According to the British consul in Alexandria, Ismāʿīl was received with "extraordinary honors, and treated by the Grand Seignior with unexampled distinction", while "the Sultan dispatched one of the principal officers of his Court with rich presents to the Viceroy".[74] One of the presents may have been the enormous diamond that the pasha was wearing when de Forbin called on him in Alexandria in early 1818. This impressed the latter more than the portrait of the sultan that the Sublime Porte also sent Muḥammad ʿAlī. The accomplished French painter dismissed this as "détestable" (execrable), while observing how rare such a picture was among the Turks.[75]

Sir Robert Liston (1742–1836), British ambassador in Istanbul (1793–96, 1811–21), also made a fuss of Ismāʿīl.[76] The latter had a reputation for being dour and arrogant, and could display gratuitous cruelty. De Forbin, who met him, noted his repellent ugliness and the low esteem in which the pasha held him.[77] In February/March 1820, over a year after Bowes

---

[72] Ibid. vii: 215, 217; Evered 2012: 630.

[73] Al-Jabartī 1958–67 vii: 222.

[74] Letter of Missett in Alexandria to Cooke of 7 July 1813 (FO 24/4), text in Burdett 2013 i: 340–4, at 340–1.

[75] De Forbin 1819: 301.

[76] Letter of Missett in Alexandria to Cooke of 7 July 1813 (FO 24/4), text in Burdett 2013 i: 343.

[77] De Forbin 1819: 310.

Wright met him, Ismāʿīl accompanied an expedition to Sudan.[78] There he enjoyed initial successes, but treated the locals harshly, to his father's anger, and was burnt alive in an uprising at Shindī in 1822.[79] Shaykh ʿAbd al-Raḥmān Āl al-Shaykh, who had been a *qāḍī* in Mecca until driven out by Ṭūsūn Pasha and was in exile in Cairo from 1819 until his return home in 1824/25, gloated over Ismāʿīl's fate decades later. He viewed it and other setbacks endured by the Egyptians as divine retribution on behalf of 'the people of Islam' (i.e. the Wahhābis).[80]

---

[78] Al-Jabartī 1958–67 vii: 463.

[79] Mengin 1823 ii: 252–3; Marsot 1984: 85–7, 206.

[80] ʿAbd al-Raḥmān Āl al-Shaykh 2005: 129–31.

CHAPTER 7

MEETINGS WITH THE CAPTIVE IMAM

Bowes Wright's encounter with Imam 'Abd Allāh

The English visitors had received permission, presumably from the pasha, for the chief interpreter to introduce them to the Wahhābi captive next day. The imam would be taken down to Shubrā on the morning of Tuesday 17 November, although the pasha would not be free to see him until the afternoon. This interpreter, whom Bowes Wright does not name, was almost certainly Boghos Yusufian (1768–1844), an Armenian, originally from Smyrna, who had once worked as a dragoman for the British consul there and had an oleaginous way with foreign visitors.[1] Now aged fifty, he enjoyed the pasha's full confidence and acted as his chief negotiator with foreign powers, which viewed him as the pasha's principal minister. It is unclear whether Briggs accompanied the visitors this time, as Bowes Wright does not mention him, but it is likely. Briggs would have known Boghos well, since the latter had personal business experience of the grain trade and advised the pasha on trade matters.[2]

---

[1] See Mengin 1823 ii: 259–63. De Forbin commented perceptively: "Cet homme, d'un caractère souple, insinuant, traite les affaires avec une finesse voisine de la fausseté. Ses manières sont caressantes, et il sait ménager tous les partis. Il parle plusieurs langues avec facilité. Son esprit est un composé de la réunion assez rare de beaucoup d'audace et de beaucoup d'astuce" [This man, with his pliant, ingratiating personality, handles business with a finesse that almost amounts to duplicity. His manners are tender, and he knows how to look after everyone. He speaks several languages fluently. His spirit is a rare blend of great boldness and much wiliness] (1819:225). Boghos did the interpreting every time de Forbin saw the pasha. Some meetings lasted several hours (ibid.: 303).

[2] Marsot 1984: 67, 76.

With Muḥammad 'Alī still occupied elsewhere, the Englishmen found the imam in a kiosk in the palace gardens. This pavilion was separate from the Shubrā Palace building. We do not have a clear picture of it or of other kiosks that existed in 1818. As previously noted, the two pavilions that survived the demolition of the main palace in the 1930s both came later: the Fountain Kiosk (Fisqiyya) featuring a rectangular colonnade, with rooms at each corner, surrounding a large marble pool or basin, in 1821; and another (Gabalāya Villa) built in 1836, which stood "on an artificial hill in a corner of the park where trees planted by the Pasha's orders veil a magnificent view of the river".[3] These kiosks may have been preceded by less ornate or elaborate structures at the same locations.

'Abd Allāh ibn Sa'ūd, accompanied by his fellow Sa'ūdi captives, was seated on a divan in the pavilion with just the *kiḥyā* bey and Ismā'īl Pasha. Aside from the Armenian Boghos Yusufian the day before, Bowes Wright and Fisher were probably the first Christians Imam 'Abd Allāh had ever met face to face, although he had corresponded with Resident William Bruce in Būshahr. Regrettably, Bowes Wright offers no record of what transpired between the Wahhābi imam and the visitors. Did they shake hands? Did the interpreter explain to the imam who Bowes Wright and his companions were? Did they converse through the interpreter? If so, was the exchange anything but awkward and stilted, given the cultural gulf between the imam and the Englishmen? How did the Wahhābi leader react to the presence of these Christian foreigners in the pasha's palace and apparently at the heart of his court? We do not know.

At least, for the benefit of Joseph Lamb and posterity, Bowes Wright painted a picture of the captive in clear colours:

> There was a slight melancholy in his countenance but mixed with a firmness and dignity suited to his situation beyond anything I had ever witnessed. His dark visage was rather long and careworn; he wore a red shawl wrapped round his head, and a loose brown and white camlet robe, and in every respect appeared, as he was, a perfect Chief of the Desert.... His Secretary and Treasurer were also present.

[3] Tugay 1963: 84. These buildings were damaged by a bombing in 2015.

The imam obviously conformed to Bowes Wright's image of a bedouin chief, even though, contrary to Western understanding of the time, Wahhābism was a small-town movement that was hostile to the bedouin, and the Āl Sa'ūd were themselves a settled, detribalised clan.[4] By contrast, the Englishman shows little sympathy for 'Abd Allāh's companions, despite their predicament, and is even unpleasantly slighting about them in the language of the era ("two cunning wretched-looking savages").

Portrait of Imam 'Abd Allāh

The description of Imam 'Abd Allāh confirms that the coloured-in drawing of the imam given in Mengin's *Histoire de l'Égypte*[5] is indeed of 'Abd Allāh as he appeared in Cairo, and not of a generic Wahhābi, as it is sometimes labelled, and that the portrait was not imagined. It is the only contemporary image we have of Imam 'Abd Allāh, or indeed of any early Sa'ūdi ruler. It gives 'Abd Allāh a moustache and beard, although the latter is shorter than implied by the other physical description we have of 'Abd Allāh shortly before his execution. This was supplied by British Ambassador Liston in Istanbul, relying on second-hand reports of sightings there a month after Bowes Wright's encounter. He told the Foreign Secretary that 'Abd Allāh was "of a middle age, a stout, well made man" with "an uncommon quantity of hair on his body, part of which was so long as to be braided all down the middle of the breast".[6] In the Cairo portrait the imam is wrapped in a brown and white woven fabric made of camel or goat hair (known as a camlet) with a red cloth around his head. This tends to suggest the drawing was based on a sighting on the same day as Bowes Wright's second visit to the palace, although 'Abd Allāh could have worn the same clothes when being paraded in the streets on the previous day.

According to the Mengin plate, the portrait is the work of Pascal Coste, the French engineer and architect. Draftsman rather than artist, he offers a flat, two-dimensional portrait of the imam with head and feet ill-proportioned and poorly aligned. There is the same poor three-

[4] Crawford 2014: 76–82.

[5] Mengin 1823: Atlas, plate 3.

[6] Letter of Sir Robert Liston to Lord Castlereagh of 24 December 1818 (FO 195/22) in Burdett 2013 i: 552.

dimensionality and lack of volume in his other amateurish drawings, some of ordinary Egyptians in everyday settings. The lithographer was Paris-based Charles Motte (1785–1836), who was later to produce lithographs for the first part of a book by Jean-François Champollion (1790–1832) entitled *Monuments de l'Égypte et de la Nubie* (1835), and whose grandson was the lithographer, artist and Egyptologist Théodule Charles Devéria (1831–71). Motte also did the plate in Mengin's *Histoire de l'Égypte* of Muḥammad 'Alī, as drawn by de Forbin in Alexandria in March 1818,[7] although de Forbin's lithographer for his own book was Horace Vernet (1789–1863), a painter of military scenes and Orientalist subjects.[8] De Forbin, who had studied under Jacques-Louis David (d. 1825) (and been a lover of Pauline Borghese, Napoleon's sister), presents the pasha in his characteristic kneeling pose, smoking a pipe – appearing much as he must have done to Bowes Wright and Fisher in Cairo six months later.

A portrait of the imam, almost identical to that by Coste, appears in monochrome in Sir Harford Jones Brydges's *A Brief History of the Wahauby*. The latter appeared in vol. II of his *An Account of the Transactions of His Majesty's Mission to the Court of Persia in the Years 1807–11*, published in London in 1834 (eleven years after Mengin's work came out in Paris). Both lithographs, with identical captions in French and English, are inaccurate in giving the year of the imam's execution as 1819. The lithographer responsible for Brydges's plate is not Motte, but the well-known Belgian Louis Haghe (1806–85 or –95), who settled in the UK in 1823 and formed the partnership Day and Haghe in 1830. He was later to supply the images for David Roberts's *The Holy Land*, etc. The name of the artist is not given in Haghe's lithograph. The drawing is basically the same, save that the ground on which 'Abd Allāh is standing is differently presented in the two images and the Haghe lithograph has the imam's head and feet better aligned. It is as if Haghe has set out to remedy some of the more obvious defects of Coste's original portrait. This may account for the absence of attribution.

It is a pity Henry Salt was not present on this occasion. A former pupil of Joseph Farington (1747–1821) and John Hoppner (1758–1810), he had once considered a career as a painter and was a fair portraitist, if a better

---

[7] Mengin 1823: Atlas: plate 1.

[8] De Forbin 1819: 224.

1. Imam ʿAbd Allāh ibn Saʿūd in Cairo in mid-November 1818, as drawn by French architect Pascal Coste. He wears the red shawl around his head and loose brown and white 'camlet' (woven outer robe), as described by Bowes Wright. Lithograph by Charles Motte, 1823.

2. The Āl Saʿūd palace in al-Dirʿiyya, the first Saʿūdi capital. The town was destroyed by Ibrāhīm Pasha after a long siege in 1818. "Ibrahim was determined to render this spot a wilderness." Photo by the visiting Sir George and Lady Rendel, March 1937.

3. The ruins of the first Saʿūdi capital as viewed from the track to Riyadh. For a short period, al-Dirʿiyya was the prosperous centre of an empire extending beyond today's Saudi Arabia. Photo by the Rendels, 1937.

4. Imam Sa'ūd seized the treasures lodged at the Prophet's tomb in this mosque in 1807, causing controversy across the Islamic world. The Ottomans arraigned his son 'Abd Allāh for this 'sacrilege' before executing him in late December 1818. Photo in the Humphrey Bowman Collection, taken before 1914.

5. In 1811, the invading Ottoman commander sent Imam Sa'ūd this sword, engraved: "From the commander of the victorious army Ṭūsūn Pasha … to the amir and leader of Najd Amir Sa'ūd ibn 'Abd al-'Azīz 1226 AH." For all the bravado, Ṭūsūn suffered a series of early defeats.

6. Panoramic view drawn by Captain William Ford, Royal Engineers, when in Cairo for the surrender of French forces in June–July 1801. Later, he invented the concept of the Martello tower.

7. A portrait by British Consul General Henry Salt of the famous Swiss explorer Jean-Louis Burckhardt, who first explained Wahhābism accurately to the West. His untimely death in 1817 deprived the lonely Salt of "almost the only *conversable* friend" he had in Cairo.

8. Portrait of Muḥammad ʿAlī Pasha by the eminent le Comte de Forbin in Alexandria in early 1818. His observations during his visit make an interesting counterpoint to those of Bowes Wright later in the year.

9. This woodcut is based on a Horace Vernet lithograph of an alert Muḥammad 'Alī watching the slaughter of the mamlūks in the citadel in 1811, while cross-legged smoking his pipe. De Forbin described the event as a remarkable piece of treachery, whereas Bowes Wright excused it as "perhaps a matter of self-defence".

10. Lithograph of Imam 'Abd Allāh, done in London 1834 by the well-known Belgian Louis Haghe, based on the Coste drawing but without attribution. Haghe may have tried to correct some of the artistic defects in Coste's portrait.

11. Portrait of Sultan Maḥmūd II in westernized military dress, done by Athanasios Karantz(ou)las in the later 19th century. The inscription describes him as '*ghāzī*' (holy warrior), a title he assumed in 1813 on recovering the Holy Cities from the Wahhābis.

12. Painted by Auguste Couder in 1840, this portrait of Muḥammad 'Alī conveys the power and wiliness of this experienced political operator. By family legend, his footstep was inaudible, whereas his son Ibrāhīm, conqueror of al-Dir'iyya, had the heavy tramp of a military man.

13. Behind this imposing gateway in Istanbul lay the grand vizier's offices, the nerve centre of the Ottoman Empire. Imam 'Abd Allāh was escorted here before being taken for interrogation and torture. Photo by Armenian official photographers to the sultan, 1880.

14. This fountain kiosk, built in 1728, lay outside the entrance to the Seraglio (Topkapi palace). Imam 'Abd Allāh was beheaded nearby. Rebels and criminals were beheaded; eminent Ottomans were strangled. Photo by Francis Bedford, 1862.

landscape artist and topographical draughtsman. In this period, most of his artistic talents were devoted to drawing monuments, with the help of various assistants.[9] His sketch in February 1817 of his new friend Jean Louis Burckhardt, who died in October of that year in Cairo, is markedly superior in quality to Coste's image of the imam.[10]

We can only speculate whether Coste drew the portrait of Imam 'Abd Allāh on his own initiative, relying on a glimpse of the captive passing through the palace grounds, or was commissioned to produce the drawing by Mengin or, less likely, by the pasha. Coste would have known Mengin as a fellow member of the small French community in Cairo. The latter had once represented French interests in Cairo on behalf of Drovetti, although he was now a minor trader.[11] With his future work on Muḥammad 'Alī in mind, Mengin may have asked Coste to produce a likeness of Imam 'Abd Allāh. Alternatively, although it is not clear that he yet thought in these terms, the pasha himself could have tasked Coste to produce a visual record of his vanquished foe and arranged for them to meet briefly during the imam's short visit to Shubrā Palace. In any event, it was probably Boghos who organised his protégé Coste's access to the imam. Coste had gone out of his way to cultivate the chief interpreter on his first arrival in Egypt in late 1817, and it was Boghos who first arranged his introduction to the pasha in January 1818.[12] Interestingly, Coste at one stage painted the interior of the historian al-Jabartī's house, probably in 1822.[13]

The pasha receives the imam

Muḥammad 'Alī and 'Abd Allāh ibn Sa'ūd had not previously met but had corresponded formally both before and after the abortive truce

[9] Halls 1834 ii: e.g. 122.

[10] Salt, who was with Burckhardt only a few hours before he died, described him as "almost the only *conversable* friend" he had in Cairo (letter to B. Richards, quoted in ibid. ii: 40). His death cast a dark shadow over the remaining years of Salt's own life (ibid. ii: 39).

[11] De Forbin mentions him as a trader at the tail end of a list of French notables in Cairo and misspells his name 'Mongin' (1819: 289). This confirms that Mengin was back in Cairo, having left in 1811. He was appointed to the consular post in Cairo again briefly in 1824.

[12] Coste 1998: 34.

[13] Jasmin 1998: 155.

negotiations in 1815.[14] 'Abd Allāh, in no position to imitate his father's calculated rudeness to Ottoman governors, had addressed him politely and with respect but without elaborate courtesies,[15] a straightforward style the pasha himself probably preferred.[16] Now, the pasha, who had previously called Imam 'Abd Allāh "cursed" in correspondence with the Sublime Porte,[17] was determined to display graciousness to his captive.

When 'Abd Allāh was taken through to him, with the Englishmen apparently in tow, Muḥammad 'Alī stood and greeted him smiling.[18] According to Mengin, the imam kissed the pasha's hand, a significant gesture in itself for a Wahhābi.[19] The Wahhābis frowned on hand-kissing as a social practice because they associated it with the submissive attitude of Sufis to their shaykhs, although they recognised it as prevalent in the Hijaz.[20] According to Bowes Wright, the pasha was highly attentive to Imam 'Abd Allāh, seating him next to him on the divan, while his son Ismā'īl and deputy Muḥammad Bey Lāẓ both remained standing out of respect. Later, Bowes Wright was to comment that "among the great in Turkey [i.e. the Ottoman Empire] the son is not allowed to sit down or take the pipe in the presence of his father, without his express permission".[21] Imam 'Abd Allāh would have recognised this custom, for a like demonstrable respect of the son for his father was traditional in Arabia too.

---

[14] See above, pp. 38–43 for the 1815 truce negotiations. Examples of the correspondence are two letters from Imam 'Abd Allāh to the pasha in 'Abd al-Raḥīm 1999: 446–8, 449–51. See above p. 40.

[15] Undated letter of Imam 'Abd Allāh to Muḥammad 'Alī, original Arabic text in 'Abd al-Raḥīm 1999: 446–8. See also Burckhardt 1831 ii: 346–7.

[16] See Marsot 1984: 93–4.

[17] Letter of 20 September 1813, Arabic translated text in 'Abd al-Raḥīm 1999: 425–32, at 426.

[18] Al-Jabartī 1958–67 vii: 447.

[19] Mengin 1823 ii: 140. According to Mengin, 'Abd Allāh had made to kiss Ibrāhīm's hand on their first meeting in al-Dir'iyya, presumably as an act of submission, but Ibrāhīm withdrew it out of modesty (ibid. ii: 132). Mengin's suggestion that 'Abd Allāh, a strict Wahhābi, smoked a pipe with Ibrāhīm (ibid. ii: 133) is not credible, since the Wahhābis banned both tobacco and the *nārjīla*. Shaykh Ḥamad ibn Nāṣir (d. 1811), the major Wahhābi jurist of the First Sa'ūdi State, declared that smoking tobacco merited forty lashes (Ibn Qāsim 1996–99: vii: 443).

[20] *Responsum* of Shaykh 'Abd al-Raḥmān ibn Ḥasan Āl al-Shaykh in Riḍā ii (1): 122–3.

[21] Letter of 31 March 1820, from Vienna.

The pasha ordered coffee and refreshments, and he and Imam ʿAbd Allāh began discussing the campaign through the interpreter, presumably Boghos. Muḥammad ʿAlī, who was culturally Ottoman, understood Arabic perfectly, but would speak only Ottoman Turkish.[22] The imam had only Arabic, which he would have spoken with a Najdi accent and usually in a dialect radically different from the Egyptian one familiar to the pasha, although he may have adopted classical Arabic for this conversation. The pasha had been illiterate on his arrival in Egypt and remained so until the age of forty-seven, i.e. until shortly before this meeting.[23] By contrast, Imam ʿAbd Allāh was well-read and had a considerable private library of more than 520 volumes, probably many inherited, which, after the fall of al-Dirʿiyya, Ibrāhīm Pasha removed to al-Madīna. There, ironically, the library, including the works of Ibn ʿAbd al-Wahhāb, was lodged at the Prophet's mosque before being transferred at the sultan's instruction to a new school in the town named for Maḥmūd II in September 1822.[24] For Bowes Wright, ʿAbd Allāh may have been a proper "Chief of the Desert", but he was much better educated than the pasha, even if no match in worldliness. Bowes Wright and Fisher, sitting at the fringes of the meeting, probably had to rely on the interpreter afterwards for a summary of their conversation, although the former observed how ʿAbd Allāh "smiled occasionally at the remarks of the Pasha".

The accounts of the meeting offered by the Cambridge Fellow and the famous Egyptian chronicler al-Jabartī of the exchanges are strikingly consistent and of similar length, while Mengin's account is almost certainly based on al-Jabartī's. Characteristically, Mengin gives no attribution.[25] Neither al-Jabartī nor Mengin mentions the presence of the English visitors. Mengin would surely have learnt of them, given the effort French and British representatives in Egypt devoted to watching each other at this period, even though he had no official standing at this point. Had there

[22] Marsot 1984: 97.

[23] Tugay 1963: 74. According to Coste, Boghos taught the pasha to read (Hill 1992: 60–1). This may help explain his closeness to, and privileged standing with, the pasha.

[24] Maktabat al-Malik ʿAbd al-ʿAzīz 2006/7: 11–12.

[25] Mengin's plagiarism from al-Jabartī (d. 1825) is covered in Verdery 1976. Mengin appears to have had no Arabic (ibid.: 338). Tagher 1950 throws light on Mengin's disagreeable personality and unsuccessful career.

been a Frenchman lurking in the background of the meeting, Mengin would not have had to rely on, and plagiarise, al-Jabartī's account.

According to al-Jabartī, the pasha opened by observing what an extended contest it had been. Imam 'Abd Allāh acknowledged the war had had its vicissitudes. Asked for an opinion of Ibrāhīm, he assured the pasha he had striven his utmost, as had the Sa'ūdis, until God had decided the outcome.[26] In Bowes Wright's account, 'Abd Allāh added that "he did not repine" at his predestined lot; "he asked for nothing for himself but recommended his country and family to his Highness' protection." Al-Jabartī and Ottoman records suggest that Muḥammad 'Alī offered to intervene with "our lord the sultan" on the imam's behalf. 'Abd Allāh replied stoically that whatever was predetermined would come to pass.[27]

There is an echo here of an interesting exchange between Ibrāhīm Pasha and 'Abd Allāh in al-Dir'iyya, as recorded by Mengin, when the imam declares, with tears welling in his eyes, that God had favoured Ibrāhīm's arms: it was not the pasha's soldiers that had defeated him; it was God who had wanted to humiliate him.[28] This suggests less fatalism, more a genuine conviction that the Wahhābis, and especially their imam, had earned divine punishment. God had shown them the true path; they had fought to implement his regime of godliness and been rewarded with military success. But at some point they had deviated and were now paying the price at the hands of a godless enemy. The imam did not look to shirk the fate that God had ordained as his penalty. This, as well as his desire to forestall a massacre and be with his people at a time of despair, may help explain why he did not flee on the fall of al-Dir'iyya, as Mengin suggests he could have done.[29] One Arabian historian described the pious leader as sacrificing himself for his people.[30]

---

26 Al-Jabartī 1958–67 vii: 447. See also Mengin 1823 ii: 140.

27 Al-Jabartī 1958–67 vii: 447; Ṣābān 2004: 118.

28 Mengin 1823 ii: 132–3. According to al-'Ajlānī, referring to an unidentified report to Paris sent by French Consul Joseph Roussel (presumably relying on a former French soldier accompanying Ibrāhīm), 'Abd Allāh reminded Ibrāhīm that God was more powerful than any of Ibrāhīm, Muḥammad 'Alī, or the sultan (1972: 15).

29 Mengin 1823 ii: 133–4.

30 Al-Rashīd 1966: 31.

The imam presents the remaining treasures to the pasha

In a move that surprised the English visitors but must have been awaited by Muḥammad ʿAlī, Imam ʿAbd Allāh produced pieces of the treasure his father had taken from the Prophet's tomb in al-Madīna in 1807. The pasha and the Ottomans were to view this dramatic surrender of the revered items into Muḥammad ʿAlī's hands as symbolic of Wahhābi capitulation. For them, the formal presentation was a gratifying piece of theatre, for the treasures were already under their effective control, as was the imam. But ʿAbd Allāh may also have seen it as a worthwhile propitiatory gesture to help assuage offence at a high-handed and provocative move by his father at the height of Saʿūdi power that had antagonised many non-Wahhābi Muslims. He was later to tell his Ottoman interrogators that he had not approved of his father's actions. He had been with his father on entering al-Madīna, but had nothing to do with the move on the tomb. He had not witnessed it and had been unhappy about it. It had even caused a breach with his father.[31]

In the words of Bowes Wright,

> These [items of treasure] were pointed out by him [ʿAbd Allāh] one by one to the Pasha; they consisted of jewels, emeralds, the holy volumes of the Koran, set with diamonds, etc. One of the emeralds was of amazing size. After this display they were put carefully into a metallic box, double locked and sealed, and delivered into the hands of the chief courier to be conveyed to Constantinople.

Al-Jabartī lists three ornate Qurans, nearly three hundred large pearls, a large emerald and a gold chain. He records Muḥammad ʿAlī querying whether this was all there was, since more had been taken from the tomb. ʿAbd Allāh replied that this was all he had found in his father's residence. He explained that Imam Saʿūd had not kept everything for himself. Bedouin chiefs, the people of al-Madīna, Ḥaram officials and the sharīf of Mecca had all had their share.[32] It is conceivable too that, on Saʿūd's death, some of the remaining treasures held by Saʿūd were handed out by ʿAbd Allāh to one or two of his uncles to induce them

[31] Zaydān 1975: 184–5.

[32] Al-Jabartī 1958–67 vii: 447.

to accept his succession.[33] Wisely, the imam did not offer the pasha the Wahhābi defence of his father's actions, especially as Imam Sa'ūd, with his famous love of splendour, had retained some items for himself. That Sa'ūd had been generous with alms for the needy of Mecca in 1807 and subsequent years would not have swayed the pasha.[34]

The pasha, who had gone through Ghālib's possessions with a toothcomb in early 1814 and laid his hands on all his assets, including cash in Yemen and (improbably) India, according to al-Jabartī,[35] confirmed that he had indeed found pieces with the deposed sharīf.[36] Although the Sa'ūdis could have used Ghālib to fence some of the jewels, since they lacked the necessary direct commercial links overseas themselves, their distrust of him makes it more likely that the notoriously grasping sharīf had bought them from Sa'ūd and then sent some of them to India on his own account.[37] As Burckhardt observed, Ghālib was actively engaged in the India trade and, on his fall, many people suspected that he had remitted considerable sums or articles of value to the East, especially to Bombay.[38] This was where many of the treasures ended up out of reach of the Ottoman recovery effort, the imam told the Ottomans under interrogation, claiming that Ghālib's son-in-law Muḥammad al-'Aṭṭās in Mecca knew all about this exercise.[39] Of the remaining items Imam Sa'ūd and selected followers kept some, while he had some of the lamps, vases, and chandeliers melted down into ingots, which he distributed to the garrison of the citadel, according to Mengin.[40] Under interrogation in Istanbul, 'Abd al-'Azīz ibn Salmān declared that the late imam also gave pieces to his sons and relations.[41]

---

33 Burckhardt says that several of Sa'ūd's brothers, including 'Abd Allāh ibn 'Abd al-'Azīz, claimed part of his wealth ("treasures") on his death (1831 ii: 288).

34 E.g. Ibn Bishr 1982–83 i: 292, 294–5, 297.

35 Al-Jabartī 1958–67 vii: 267. See also Burckhardt 1831 ii: 261.

36 Al-Jabartī 1958–67 vii: 447.

37 As suggested by 'Abd al-'Azīz ibn Salmān under interrogation (Zaydān 1975: 185).

38 Burckhardt 1831 ii: 263; De Gaury 1951: 207.

39 Zaydān 1975: 184.

40 Mengin 1823 ii: 535–6.

41 Zaydān 1975: 185.

Mengin reports that Sa'ūd put the jewels to public auction, where they were sold to local inhabitants and foreigners at depressed prices well below their true value. Ghālib and some of the other local notables may have acquired the valuables this way. What remains unclear from the sources is the extent to which the proceeds from the sales were given by Sa'ūd to the treasury (the *bayt al-māl*, based in a large building near the Āl Sa'ūd Palace in the al-Ṭurayf quarter of al-Dir'iyya) to be devoted to warfare against unbelievers, the poor of the Holy Cities, support for clerics, or other charitable objects, consistent with later Wahhābi justifications for his seizure and disposal of the treasures. Ottoman sources naturally imply that Imam Sa'ūd purloined them all for his own aggrandisement or to secure the support of his henchmen.

The presentation concluded, Muḥammad 'Alī Pasha ended the meeting by granting Imam 'Abd Allāh a robe of honour. The gift of robes or clothes was a traditional mark of appreciation and a reward for meritorious service, as well as a currency to recruit individuals to one's cause, much deployed by the pasha with the bedouin at the start of the Hijaz war. Before launching the campaign, he was careful to spell out his bribery requirements to the Sublime Porte. Aside from large sums for senior officers and soldiers, and the usual *ṣurra*s and gifts for the tribes, the inhabitants of the Holy Cities, and the sharīf, he sought a large number of choice garments to give tribal leaders and notables, including Kashmiri shawls and furs.[42]

On this occasion, the gift of a robe served as a natural, if ostentatious, gesture of generosity to a defeated adversary with only weeks to live. Perhaps as part of a peace overture, Imam 'Abd Allāh had himself sent Ṭūsūn Pasha a present of clothes in April/May 1815 before the short-lived truce "by way of friendship and to maintain relations",[43] while in 1811 Ṭūsūn had presented Imam Sa'ūd with a sword.[44] The pasha intended to demonstrate his regard for his dignified but doomed visitor. This respect may have been tinged with regret at sending 'Abd Allāh to

[42] Attachment Muḥammad 'Alī's letter to the Sublime Porte of 9 March 1808, Arabic translated text in 'Abd al-Rahīm 1999: 368–73.

[43] Letter of Imam 'Abd Allāh to Ṭūsūn Pasha of April/May 1815, held by KFCRIS in Riyadh. Mengin mentions Imam 'Abd Allāh sending generous presents during the peace negotations as evidence of his good faith (1823 ii: 56; see also ibid. ii: 67).

[44] This sword, held by the KFCRIS, is shown in Plate 5.

his certain death in Istanbul. Yet Muḥammad ʿAlī viewed execution as the fitting end for defeated enemies, and reasons of state demanded the prisoner's immediate despatch to the sultan.

The pasha and the imam depart

Rather than lingering to savour the moment, the pasha seems to have been in a hurry to leave. Directly after the ceremony, he boarded his *cangia* (a two-masted sailing boat with a cabin) for Damietta. Bowes Wright observed his mamlūks galloping after him along the river banks. The pasha did not even stop to write an accompanying explanatory letter about the treasures to the sultan, nor to Muḥammad Najīb, his long-time representative in Istanbul, who had escorted the previous doomed ʿUthmān al-Muḍāifī from Cairo to Istanbul five years before.[45]

Leaving the Shubrā Palace in turn, the captive imam returned to the residence of Ismāʿīl Pasha in Būlāq.[46] On the following day, Wednesday 18 November, even as Bowes Wright was penning an account of his experiences in Egypt to Joseph Lamb, ʿAbd Allāh and his attendants were on their way to Alexandria escorted by the Ottoman chief courier (*taṭar āghā*) and associates to board a ship for Istanbul.[47] The sultan was impatient for delivery of his trophy. The grand vizier's deputy wrote to the pasha on 24 November, reminding him of his promise to send Imam ʿAbd Allāh in response to the sultan's order and urging speed.[48] By then, the imam was already well on his way to the Ottoman capital, where his arrival was eagerly awaited.[49] In Istanbul, he was not to be accorded the courtesy shown to him as a defeated foe by Muḥammad ʿAlī in Cairo. For the Ottomans, the Wahhābi leader had the status of a mere criminal, to be tortured, humiliated, executed, and deprived of proper burial.

---

45 Al-Jabartī 1958–67 vii: 227. See p. 29 above.

46 Ibid. vii: 447; Mengin 1823 ii: 140. Mengin's record of the encounter is almost certainly an example of him plagiarising al-Jabartī, since he inserts mention of the robe of honour and Imam ʿAbd Allāh's return to Ismāʿīl Pasha's house before relating the production of the jewels, just as al-Jabartī does.

47 Al-Jabartī, 1958–67 vii: 448.

48 Letter of Kiḥyā Adīb to Muḥammad ʿAlī of 24 November 1818 in ʿAbd al-Raḥīm 1983: 673–5, at 674–5.

49 Letter of Muḥammad Najīb to Muḥammad ʿAlī of 24 December 1818 in ʿAbd al-Raḥīm 1983: 678–9, at 678.

Any encounter between a victor and his vanquished enemy after a long and brutal war carries symbolic and historic importance. Yet there is also invariably an element of human poignancy in the personal situation of the captive leader, especially when his life is already forfeit. Ripped from his overrun capital, isolated, uncertain of the fate of his family and followers, and powerless in the face of his captors' whims, Imam 'Abd Allāh must have found his journey to Cairo, and then Istanbul, both interminable and too short. In describing "a slight melancholy in his countenance but mixed with a firmness and dignity suited to his situation beyond anything I had ever witnessed", Bowes Wright, with his customary sensibility, helps to restore the moving human dimension to the doomed imam's story. Perhaps inevitably, for all al-Jabartī's obvious sympathy for him, that is largely missing from second-hand accounts and those written long after the event. But Bowes Wright was there and a direct witness to the imam's composure and courage. Imam 'Abd Allāh would need to draw on his full reserves of faith and fortitude to face the next and final ordeal in the Ottoman capital.

CHAPTER 8

Torture and Execution in Istanbul

From the quay to the Sublime Porte

Imam ʿAbd Allāh's party arrived by ship in the Ottoman capital on 14 December, docking at the chief *daftardār*'s (treasurer's) quay by the mosque of Abū Ayyūb al-Anṣārī (Eyüp Sulṭān). This mosque, dating back to 1458, was the traditional site for the coronation of Ottoman sultans and had been rebuilt as recently as 1798–1800. Muḥammad Najīb Effendi, Muḥammad ʿAlī's representative at the Sublime Porte, was on the quay with the municipal police chief, palace guards sent by the Ottoman grand vizier under the captain of the guard, and other Ottoman officials.[1] Receiving the metal strongbox under Muḥammad ʿAlī's seal from the courier accompanying Imam ʿAbd Allāh, Najīb faced a quandary in that he was unsure of the contents. Later, having opened the box and established what was inside, he hastened to forward the resealed container to the Sublime Porte with an explanatory note.[2]

Armed guards flanked the imam and his companions as they tramped in chains the considerable distance from the quay to Divan Yolu, the main processional street of the Ottoman Empire (today's Divan Yolu Caddesi in the Fatih district of Istanbul). They were taken first to the prison, where they were fettered, and then, surrounded by guards, to the offices of the Sublime Porte, nerve-centre of the Ottoman state. The streets through which they passed were crowded. The captives' imminent

[1] Cevdet 1874 xi: 59.

[2] Zaydān 1975: 190.

arrival had been well-signalled by messengers, and people were eager to glimpse the one-time leader of defeated rebels.[3] The Ottomans were as keen as Muḥammad ʿAlī to milk the victory over the Wahhābis, who had defied them and undermined their religious legitimacy, to boost their prestige and deter others. The success was especially important for Sultan Maḥmūd II, who still faced conservative forces resistant to his reforms, especially in the military field.

On the prisoners' arrival at the Sublime Porte, Meḥmed Pasha (1765–1837), grand vizier 1818–20, celebrated their delivery by distributing valuable gifts to Muḥammad Najīb, senior officials, the chief courier, several naval captains, and guard commanders.[4] He then gave orders for the captives to be taken to the cells of the palace guard commander (*bostancıbaşı*), who was equal in rank to a pasha and also acted as chief executioner.[5] There they were interrogated separately for three days by Pertev Effendi (presumably Meḥmed Pertev [1785–1837]) and the official interpreter for the Holy Places (*tarjumān al-ḥaramayn*) on the sultan's behalf.[6]

It is notable that the grand vizier had strong Sufi affiliations with the Mevlevi (Rūmī) order, which the sultan himself favoured, while Pertev belonged to the Naqshbandi order,[7] which was deeply hostile to Wahhābism. From the start, the Wahhābis had condemned Sufi spiritual beliefs, practices, and hierarchies, regarding them as an affront to the oneness of God (*tawḥīd*). In response, some Sufis spearheaded the first diatribes against the Wahhābis in the early 1740s. In view of such

[3] Letter of Muḥammad Najīb to Muḥammad ʿAlī of 24 December 1818 in ʿAbd al-Raḥīm 1983: 678–9, at 678.

[4] These awards included an outer garment of sable fur for each, while the associates and servants of the chief courier and the officers of his ship were cloaked in robes of honour. The chief courier received a full state salary with an interest of five purses (*kise*) per year, while his associates and servants and the naval captains and officers were given bounty from the treasury commensurate with rank (Cevdet 1874 xi: 59–60). See also letter of Muḥammad Najīb to Muḥammad ʿAlī of 24 December 1818, in ʿAbd al-Raḥīm 1983: 678–9. By a strange irony, Meḥmed Pasha was to die in Yanbuʿ, the port from which Imam ʿAbd Allāh crossed the Red Sea to Suez on his final journey.

[5] Cevdet 1874 xi: 60.

[6] As Pertev Pasha, he was minister of interior 1835–37. He was bowstrung on the sultan's orders in 1837 for criticising him outspokenly. Pertev drafted the famous decree announcing the abolition of the Janissary Corps in 1826.

[7] Abu-Manneh 1982: 21, 25.

mutual antagonism, it is striking that Imam 'Abd Allāh's interrogation, as recorded, focused on missing treasures and did not address issues of creed or ideology. Whether there is other evidence in Ottoman archives to corroborate a contemporary traveller's suggestion that Ottoman *'ulamā'* tried unavailingly to convert the Wahhābi leader to their religious viewpoint is a question that awaits further research.[8]

Sultan Maḥmūd took a close personal interest in the questioning of the Wahhābis. The interrogators promised them better treatment in return for honest, reliable answers, and pressed the captives repeatedly on the fate of all the valuable items taken by Imam Sa'ūd and his entourage from the Prophet's mosque in 1807, the shrine of Imām Ḥusayn in Karbalā' in 1802, and other holy places. Where were all these treasures? Who had them? Sometimes the Ottoman officials employed persuasion, at others times violence (as they admitted to the sultan), but to no avail. Imam 'Abd Allāh denied repeatedly that he had been present on either occasion in al-Madīna or Karbalā' or ever handled any of the treasures, and swore on oath that he had no idea who had taken them. He had not even been in Karbalā' with his father. He was obdurate in insisting that the only people alive who knew what had happened to the missing items from al-Madīna and Karbalā' were named associates of his late father, now Ibrāhīm Pasha's prisoners in al-Dir'iyya. He claimed he had personally disapproved of the al-Madīna episode, which had estranged him from his father.

'Abd al-'Azīz, his assistant secretary, corroborated this line. On the other hand, like the valet, he could offer nothing on the plundering of the shrines. The Ottoman interrogators, who did not believe 'Abd Allāh's repeated protestations of innocence, made no progress in extracting a confession. In the words of their official report, "the pen dried". The sultan, keen to recover the treasures and assuage the anger of the shah at the despoiling of Karbalā', was disappointed. He noted to the grand vizier that, if these 'evil men' knew any more than they were saying, they were not saying it, and gave orders for Muḥammad 'Alī and Ibrāhīm Pasha to make further enquiries.[9]

---

[8] Rottiers 1829: 341.

[9] Zaydān 1975: 182–5 (at 182, giving the text and Arabic translation of document 19601, an undated exchange between the sultan and the grand vizier. I have relied on the Arabic translation).

Arraignment and execution

After three days of questioning in their cells, and accompanied by a crowd of idlers, the three Saʿūdis were led by the palace guard in their red skull caps to Eski Saray, the old imperial palace completed in 1458 that was located near Beyazit Square in today's Fatih district, of which nothing survives today. The sultan was to be present, and we can assume that he processed to the Eski Saray with some pomp. De Forbin, in Istanbul the year before (28 September–15 October 1817), offers a description of the sultan on his way to Friday prayers, noting the ceremonial that attended his progress:

> Le sultan Mahmoud, suivi d'un cortége [*sic* ; cortège] immense, traverse cette foule pour se rendre à la prière du vendredi. Je le vis monté sur un cheval blanc, caparaçonné d'un tissu d'or et de perles, et dont les harnais sont chargés de diamans [*sic* ; diamants]. Le Grand-Seigneur me parut avoir trente ans à peine. Sa figure est pâle, noble et régulière. Il promenait sur son peuple de grands yeux noirs, dont les regards étaient accueillis par le silence le plus profond. Le sultan était déjà loin, des cris de réjouissance annonçaient son entrée dans la mosquée d'Ayoub, et le front des fidèles Osmanlis touchait encore la poussière.[10]

Ambassador Liston, writing on Christmas Eve 1818, said of the Wahhābi captives in the Eski Saray:

> [there] they underwent a short examination before the principal members of the Diwan in the presence of His Highness himself, who was seated in an open gallery on the first floor of the building, overlooking the assembly. At the same time, the persons of the prisoners were searched, and there were found on the leader a seal

[10] De Forbin 1819: 44–5: "The sultan, followed by a great cortege, moved through this throng to attend Friday prayers. I saw him mounted on a white horse, with trappings in fabric woven with gold and pearls and a harness decorated with diamonds. The Grand Seigneur appeared to be scarcely thirty years old. His face was pale and noble, with regular features. He surveyed his people with large black eyes, and his glances were greeted by a deep silence. Even when the sultan was some distance off, cries of joy announced his arrival at the Ayoub mosque and the foreheads of loyal Ottomans touched the dust again."

> on which were engraved the words – Abdullah, son of Soo-ood, Caliph, besides two precious stones of a very large size, the one said to be a Ruby, the other an Emerald, understood to be a part of the booty carried off from Mecca [*sic*; al-Madīna], when that place was pillaged by the Wahabees. The chief said that the rest of the spoil had been divided among his followers.[11]

The subsequent verdict and sentence that issued from the imperial divan (Diwān-i Hümayun), which included the grand vizier and the shaykh al-Islām, were a foregone conclusion. Even though he had denied steadfastly participating in the raid on the tomb and indeed claimed it had alienated him from his father, Imam ʿAbd Allāh was found guilty of the theft of the treasures by his father and himself.[12] The sin of the father was visited on the son. For all the Ottoman offers of clemency, he can have expected nothing but execution. Beheading was the traditional Ottoman method with external opponents or rebels; strangling was a privilege reserved for Ottoman family members or high-ranking officials.[13] The imam's underlings, assistant secretary ʿAbd al-ʿAzīz and valet ʿAbd Allāh, might have hoped to have avoided sharing his fate, but received no clemency. Once proud of having been picked out by the imam in Cairo to accompany him on his onward journey, they now rued this bitterly.[14]

The seal naming him caliph was clearly planted on ʿAbd Allāh by the Ottomans. The imam's own seal carried the simple inscription "*al-wāthiq bi-allāh al-wudūd ʿAbd Allāh bin Saʿūd al-Saʿūd*" ("Trusting in God, the devoted ʿAbd Allāh ibn Saʿūd al-Saʿūd"). Throughout the conflict the Ottomans persistently alleged a Saʿūdi claim to the caliphate, a view Muḥammad ʿAlī also purveyed.[15] This was pure invention and propaganda, since the Saʿūdi rulers and Wahhābi clerics never advanced one. The Wahhābis' removal of mention of the sultan's name from Friday prayers in Najd

[11] Letter of Liston to Castlereagh of 24 December 1818 (FO 195/22) in Burdett 2013 i: 551. The underlinings are Liston's.

[12] Kūrshūn 2005: 94, n. 288.

[13] In Britain the convention until the mid-18th century was the reverse. Noblemen were beheaded and common people hanged.

[14] As ʿAbd al-ʿAzīz commented to his interrogators (Zaydān 1975: 185).

[15] E.g. letter to the Sublime Porte of 20 September 1813, Arabic translated text in ʿAbd al-Raḥīm 1999: 425–32, at 427.

and then in the Hijaz had nothing to do with a countervailing claim to the caliphate, since, as we have seen, they were averse to any reference to rulers, including the Āl Saʿūd, in those prayers. But they were dismissive of the Ottomans' assertion of the caliphate, which the Sublime Porte had reinvigorated only in the 1770s, thanks to territorial losses in the Caucasus to Russia.

Because of religious practices in the empire, the Wahhābis held Ottoman dominions to be the land of unbelief. Rather than engage on this issue, it suited the Ottomans to misrepresent and distort the nature of the Wahhābi religious challenge. They hinged their verdict on ʿAbd Allāh on an alleged single act of plunder committed by his father, ignoring the religious justification offered by the local *muftī*s, including the one representing the Ottomans' own Ḥanafi school of law. As for the ruby and emerald allegedly found on ʿAbd Allāh, these were presumably stones already back in Ottoman possession that officials planted on ʿAbd Allāh and produced at Eski Saray for dramatic effect.

The three men were paraded through the streets with chains around their necks, treated with contempt by their escort, and hooted and cursed by many of the spectators. This was a public exhibition they apparently had to endure for three days.[16] They displayed "steadiness and apparent tranquillity", according to Liston. The condemned but outwardly calm Saʿūdi imam was beheaded, possibly by a palace guard or janissary, at the courtyard gate of the Seraglio (Bāb-i Hümayun) on about 20 December 1818. His companions were beheaded on the same day in different squares or open spaces elsewhere in the city, according to the British ambassador.[17] The Ottoman historian says they were all executed in front of Yalı Köşk, a structure in Topkapi Palace close to the *bostancıbaşı*'s dungeon.[18] The Russian embassy reported the Wahhābi leader as beheaded in front of the main gate of St Sophia, ʿAbd al-ʿAzīz ibn Salmān ('the minister') decapitated outside the palace, and ʿAbd Allāh al-Sirrī ('the imam') in one of the main markets. It added that

[16] Ottoman records point to three successive days of parading for the captives (e.g. Ṣābān 2004: 118).

[17] Letter of Liston to Castlereagh of 24 December 1818 (FO 195/22) in Burdett 2013: i 551–2. It is unclear why Rottiers dates the execution to November 1818, especially since he claimed almost to have witnessed the event (Rottiers 1829: 340).

[18] Cevdet 1874 xi: 60.

"their bodies were displayed with their heads under their arms … and were thrown into the sea three days later".[19]

There was thus to be no proper religious burial for the three Wahhābis. The Ottoman practice was to place the severed heads of executed criminals by the Bāb-i Hümayun and then have the corpses thrown into the sea after three days, unless someone paid for permission to bury them.[20] The privilege of the First Court of Topkapi Palace was reserved for the heads or body parts of errant (or unlucky) Ottoman family members or notables, before these were duly interred. The Wahhābi practice for rulers and common people alike was (and remains) an unmarked grave, but 'Abd Allāh was deprived even of this.

A comment in the *The Times* of London of 9 January 1819 referred to a Constantinople report recording the victory over the Wahhābis: "The Chief of the sect, Abdulla Ben Suud, was taken alive, and was on his way to Constantinople, in chains – 'an ample indemnity', it is coolly observed, 'for the head of the Hospodar of Wallachia, which has escaped the iron spikes at the gate of the Seraglio'. One head is as good as another, no doubt, to the admirers of such exhibitions." By a curious juxtaposition, this caustic aside on Ottoman practices followed spirited criticism of those who considered cruel British treatment of the imprisoned Bonaparte on St Helena. In a dig at the Whigs, the paper pronounced: "Every measure is declared cruel by these men, which deprives their idol of the means of again becoming what he once was." Muḥammad 'Alī, once puzzled at the British sparing Napoleon after Waterloo, would have regarded the worry about a dangerous enemy's capacity for political resurrection as sufficient reason to dispose of him once and for all. Within a few years, he was himself to discover that beheading Imam 'Abd Allāh contributed little towards eliminating the Wahhābi movement.

On 6 February 1819, *The Times*, relying on a report from the *Dutch and Flanders Mail*, itself based on intelligence from Istanbul of 24 December, commented as follows on this "series of inhuman, though not unlooked-for, spectacles exhibited at Constantinople, on the 16th of December, and the following days":

---

[19] Vassiliev 1998:155, quoting from the Archives of Russian Foreign Policy.

[20] MacMichael 1819: 166–7.

> The chief of the Wechabites and his Minister [*sic*],[21] who had been expected for some time, were then brought in chains to the Turkish capital, and led through the streets in barbarous triumph. They were then sent to prison and put to the torture; they were afterwards beheaded *in the* SULTAN'*s presence*, their bodies exposed during three days, and finally delivered up to be torn in pieces by the populace. Such horrors are scarcely to be conceived but in a country which is inaccessible to the progress of civilization.

Interestingly, the original *Dutch and Flanders Mail* account summarised in the same issue does not say explicitly that they were beheaded in front of the sultan, nor that the populace tore the corpses apart. *The Times* seems to have used editorial licence to make a sweeping point about the perceived backwardness of the Ottoman Empire (and Islam). This presumption of cultural and moral superiority would probably not have been endorsed or appreciated by the Fellow of Jesus College, who relished "sojourning among the noble citizens of the world, men who despise the differences of place and education, but see in all something to please and to admire".

Ambassador Liston described the condemned imam as meeting "with the fate which Sultan Mahmut seems to reserve for all his enemies who happen to come within the reach of his power".[22] It was to demonstrate that reach to the inhabitants of his capital and foreign observers that Sultan Maḥmūd had the imam brought to Istanbul, paraded in demeaning fashion, and decapitated. There was widespread rejoicing. The Russians recorded the sultan as celebrating with prayers of thanks throughout the empire, the release of imprisoned debtors, the promise that the state would pay their creditors, and the distribution of large sums at mosques and *madrasa*s (religious schools).[23] Sultan Maḥmūd was resolved that as many of his subjects as possible should become aware of his triumph and have cause to remember it.

As for the recovered treasures, they were logged in a register at the Sublime Porte, repaired, and restored to the Prophet's tomb by the

---

[21] Elsewhere on the same page he is described as the chief's 'Imam'.

[22] Letter of Liston to Castlereagh of 24 December 1818 (FO 195/22) in Burdett 2013 i: 550.

[23] Vassiliev 1999: 155.

official accompanying the *ṣurra* on the sultan's instructions.[24] Perhaps to help reduce the embarrassment of the tomb's despoliation and remedy its comparative bareness, Sultan Maḥmūd and his immediate family did much to replenish the inventory. He proved one of the most generous of all the donors, although his wives and daughter outdid him. Muḥammad 'Alī Pasha, one of his wives, and a widow of Ṭūsūn Pasha also contributed, but less generously.[25] Sultan Maḥmūd also had the cupola over the Prophet's tomb restored.

News of the imam's execution arrived back in Cairo on 4 March 1819, arousing sympathy for the condemned men in chronicler al-Jabartī. Controversially, he describes them as martyrs (*shuhadā'*),[26] whereas the official Ottoman position was that those killed fighting the Wahhābis were the martyrs. Back in a chaotic and fragmented Najd, there was widespread popular uncertainty about the late imam's fate for years to come, as conflicting rumours circulated about what had happened to him.[27] If Shaykh 'Abd al-Raḥmān ibn Ḥasan tried, on his return to Najd in 1825/26, to settle the matter and end such speculation, there is no record of it. Unfortunately, though a prolific producer of *fatwā*s and religious tracts, he never wrote a memoir or history, beyond a few recollections folded into his teaching manual *al-Maqāmāt*. He was not prepared to dwell further on a period of defeat and humiliation.

---

24 Cevdet 1874 xi: 60; Kūrshūn 2005: 93, n. 284; Zaydān 1975: 190.

25 Ṣābān 2005: 4, 6–8, 22, 26–7, 40–1, 48–9, 63.

26 Al-Jabartī 1958–67 vii: 452. De Forbin heard that the imam had died under hideous tortures (1819: 287, n.1).

27 See al-Rashīd 1966: 31.

CHAPTER 9

Āl Sa‘ūd and Āl al-Shaykh Exiled to Cairo

Imam ‘Abd Allāh was far from the last Wahhābi despatched to Egypt by Ibrāhīm Pasha, but he was the last one to be transported through Cairo as an exhibit and then beheaded in Istanbul. Ibrāhīm executed a few captured Wahhābis in cold blood in al-Dir‘iyya directly after its fall. Most notoriously, he killed the premier ideologue of the late First Sa‘ūdi State and hardline opponent of the invading Ottomans, Sulaymān ibn ‘Abd Allāh Āl al-Shaykh, oldest son of the moderate head of the religious establishment.[1] But these select individuals appear to have earned his personal resentment and hatred. Having secured and staged his exhibition of victory in Cairo, Muḥammad ‘Alī Pasha was not interested in slaughtering his erstwhile enemies wholesale as he had the mamlūks.

To prevent the Wahhābis threatening his interests further, the pasha was determined not only to destroy the Sa‘ūdi capital but to exile all remaining members of the Āl Sa‘ūd and descendants of Ibn ‘Abd al-Wahhāb (Āl al-Shaykh) to Cairo. His forces worked to round them up in Najd, al-Aḥsā’ and elsewhere. The pasha told Ibrāhīm to send the remaining brothers of Imam ‘Abd Allāh (Fahad, Sa‘d, Ḥasan and Khālid) and other notables into Egyptian exile. Large armed escorts took them to Yanbu‘, probably via al-Madīna, for the sea transit to Suez.[2] They were supposed to arrive there by late April when the governor received orders

[1] Ibn Bishr 1982–83 i: 424.

[2] Mengin 1823 ii: 151.

from Muḥammad ʿAlī to take good care of them.[3] The deportees would have worried that they were about to share the fate of their late imam.

Already on 24 March, an emissary from the Sublime Porte had announced in Cairo an imperial edict granting remaining Wahhābis amnesty and lavishing praise on Muḥammad ʿAlī.[4] There was a flood of congratulatory letters to the pasha from senior Ottoman dignitaries from across the empire who relished knowing that Imam ʿAbd Allāh had been delivered to Istanbul in shackles. The pasha would have been particularly gratified to receive an effusive letter in rhyming Arabic prose from Persian Crown Prince ʿAbbās Mirzā (d. 1833), delivered by Persian ambassador Sayyid ʿAlī Khān after the fall of al-Dirʿiyya. This lauded his achievement in fighting 'the Arabs' (i.e. nomads) and calling him 'warrior in the cause of religion' (*ghāzī fī sabīl al-dīn*). As a mark of appreciation, ʿAbbās Mirzā forwarded to him an ancient sword that had been handed down by Persian kings.[5] The Persians also sent a delegation that arrived in Cairo in July/August 1820 with further presents for the pasha, including horses.[6]

On 13 May 1819, the first major group of nearly four hundred Wahhābis, including senior members of the Āl Saʿūd and Āl al-Shaykh with their women and children, finally arrived in Cairo. They took up residence at a barracks in al-Azbakiyya. A son of the executed imam with his entourage occupied a house by the 14th-century al-Sitt Miska mosque in the al-Sayyida Zaynab district.[7] The most prominent Wahhābi in the group was Shaykh ʿAbd Allāh, son of Ibn ʿAbd al-Wahhāb. He had been head of the Wahhābi religious establishment since at least 1809 and from Cairene exile continued to supply *responsa* to the queries of Najdi notables.[8] He was accompanied by his less prominent brothers ʿAlī and Ibrāhīm. It had been ʿAlī, then on campaign with Imam ʿAbd Allāh, who

---

[3] Letter from Muḥammad ʿAlī to the governor of Suez of 28 April 1819, in ʿAbd al-Raḥīm 1983: 691–2, reflecting the pasha's close interest in the detainees' treatment and state of mind.

[4] Al-Jabartī 1958–67 vii: 453. The amnesty was announced by Qahwajī Pasha, who also brought magnificent gifts for Muḥammad ʿAlī and Ibrāhīm. He was duly deluged with gifts when he left (ibid. vii: 455).

[5] Undated letter in ʿAbd al-Raḥīm 1999: 452–4.

[6] Al-Jabartī 1958–67 vii: 468.

[7] Ibid. vii: 455. Four sons of ʿAbd Allāh were taken at al-Dirʿiyya.

[8] *Responsum* of ʿAbd al-Raḥmān ibn Ḥasan in Riḍā 1928 i: 332.

had overseen the swearing of allegiance (*bay'a*) to him when news came of Imam Sa'ūd's demise.[9] All of these Āl al-Shaykh and 'Abd Allāh's son 'Abd al-Raḥmān were to die in exile in Cairo. Shaykh 'Abd Allāh's nephew, 'Abd al-Raḥmān ibn Ḥasan and his young son 'Abd al-Laṭīf (d. 1876) both returned to Najd, the former in 1825/26 and the latter in 1847/48, to become successive heads of the religious establishment during the Second Sa'ūdi State.

The exiles were free to come and go and visit the Egyptian *'ulamā'* among others, as well as do their shopping.[10] They would have particularly appreciated access to libraries and bookshops. The Wahhābis had always been energetic collectors of books and the delegates in 1815 had been active in acquiring religious works during their stay, though disappointed to learn that their Ḥanbali school of law had long since died out in Cairo.[11] Even if Ḥanbali jurisprudence (*fiqh*) was no longer taught, there were other Islamic sciences and non-religious subjects on offer at al-Azhar. During his six years in Cairo, Shaykh 'Abd al-Raḥmān was taught by historian al-Jabartī, among numerous others, and may have been responsible for the latter's understanding of, and sympathy towards, Wahhābism.[12] He was probably also the major source for Mengin's *Précis de l'histoire de Wahaby*,[13] especially as he appears to have been active, well-networked in Cairo, and, as a past pupil of early Wahhābi chronicler Ibn Ghannām, familiar with the latter's history, on which the *Précis* seems to be roughly based. Through such contacts, these exiles would have received detailed descriptions of the ill-fated imam's transit of the city and his exchanges with Muḥammad 'Alī, even if they chose not to relay or recycle these accounts to those cut off from reliable information in Najd.

One of the more colourful Wahhābi *'ulamā'* to arrive in Cairo was Aḥmad ibn Ḥusayn ibn Rashīd ibn 'Afāliq (*ca.* 1763/64–1841/42), known as Aḥmad al-Ḥanbalī. Originally an anti-Wahhābi from al-Aḥsā', he agitated in al-Madīna for Ottoman assistance against the Sa'ūdis. When Sa'ūd entered al-Madīna in 1806, Aḥmad impressed him as a cleric of

---

[9] Ibn Bishr 1982–83 i: 368.

[10] Al-Jabartī 1958–67 vii: 455.

[11] Ibid. vii: 319.

[12] 'Abd al-Raḥmān ibn Ḥasan's record of his teachers is in Riḍā 1928 ii (1): 20–4, at 21.

[13] Mengin 1823 ii: 449–544. See Bonacina 2015: 150–1, n. 64.

sound beliefs, a measure of the cleric's capacity for deception, according to one anti-Wahhābi biographer.[14] Sa'ūd confirmed him as a teacher at the Prophet's mosque and made him a *qāḍī*.[15] He taught Wahhābi doctrine and, thanks to Sa'ūd's respect for him, acquired influence with the Sa'ūdi authorities in al-Madīna, which he tried to exploit to protect locals' interests.[16] After the Ottoman forces arrived, he retreated to al-Dir'iyya to teach and became a close associate of Imam Sa'ūd, according to Imam 'Abd Allāh under Ottoman interrogation, who said he was one of the half-dozen to enter the Prophet's tomb with the imam.[17] 'Abd Allāh deployed him to seek peace with Ibrāhīm Pasha, but the latter rejected the approach and took offence at Aḥmad's tone with him.[18] Aḥmad was taken prisoner just before the final fall of al-Dir'iyya. Ibrāhīm had him tortured and beaten, and all his teeth torn out, apparently just before Imam 'Abd Allāh's departure for Cairo.[19] The cleric was rescued by Muḥammad 'Alī, who invited him to Cairo, gave him funding, and made him shaykh (i.e. *muftī*) of the Ḥanbalis. In a propitiatory gesture that served as a reproach to Ibrāhīm, the pasha even asked him to do readings to his household in the citadel and at his home. He taught at al-Azhar and eventually died in Cairo in 1841/42.[20]

Further Wahhābis arrived late in 1819 and resided at a house in 'Abidīn.[21] Then more women and children arrived at the turn of the year and settled in al-Humāyīl. They immediately set about selling the slaves that had accompanied them to whoever might buy them, even though these slaves were Muslims and originally free.[22] This was the point at which Ibrāhīm Pasha himself returned to Cairo amid much celebration Finally, a further group arrived chained on camels in July 1821, after being

---

[14] Ibn Ḥumayd 1989: 59; Āl Bassām 1998/99 i: 457–66, at 459–60.

[15] Ibn Bishr 1982–83 i: 364.

[16] Ibn Ḥumayd 1989: 59–60.

[17] Zaydān 1975: 184.

[18] Mengin 1823 ii: 136.

[19] Letter of Muḥammad 'Alī to the Sublime Porte of 11 September 1818, Arabic translated text in Mawjānī 2014: 426–9, at 428; Ibn Bishr 1982–83 i: 421.

[20] Ibn Ḥumayd 1989: 60.

[21] Al-Jabartī 1958–67 vii: 458.

[22] Ibid. vii: 459.

involved with Mishārī ibn Sa'ūd and Imam Sa'ūd's brother 'Umar ibn 'Abd al-'Azīz in an unsuccessful effort to re-establish the Sa'ūdi state that had the Ottomans worried. 'Umar himself, his sons, and nephews were among the party. 'Umar had originally been dispatched by Ibrāhīm Pasha to Egypt, but gave his escort the slip in a village near Yanbu' and returned to al-Dir'iyya after Ibrāhīm had left. He was joined there by Mishārī ibn Sa'ūd, who called on Najdis to give obedience. The two men sought to rally the Āl Sa'ūd, but Ḥusayn Bey put a swift stop to their campaign. He captured Mishārī, who died en route to Egyptian exile, and seized 'Umar and his sons after besieging them for a few days in the citadel in Riyadh until they surrendered. The future Imam Turkī ibn 'Abd Allāh (d. 1834) slipped away into the night. 'Umar and his group ended up inhabiting the al-Ḥanafi district of Cairo close to the previous batches of exiles, while Turkī went on to re-establish Sa'ūdi rule.[23]

We do not have a reliable total figure for the number of Sa'ūdi and Wahhābi notables transported to Egypt. Khalīl al-Rajabī, a contemporary Egyptian historian, who was writing to glorify Muḥammad 'Alī (and, as a Sufi of the Shādhili order, was fervently anti-Wahhābi), suggests nearly a thousand men arrived from Najd in only two groups, accompanied by their women and children.[24] The pasha would have been confident that he had effectively decapitated the local Wahhābi order. It was indeed to be just a small nucleus of this captive population from the Āl Sa'ūd and Āl al-Shaykh, together with some who had eluded Ibrāhīm Pasha's clutches in Najd, that reconstituted the Sa'ūdi state on a more modest scale than its predecessor. Others in the exiled community in Cairo found it hard to keep the Wahhābi faith and preserve their Najdi affiliations and links. Relatively few escaped back to Arabia, and most gradually became assimilated into Egyptian society. A few later even proved ready to serve Muḥammad 'Alī's interests in Arabia.

After nearly twenty fruitless years of trying to control Najd, Muḥammad 'Alī resorted to one of Imam 'Abd Allāh's younger brothers, Khālid ibn Sa'ūd, as his instrument in Central Arabia, hoping that he might command the following of his father and brother and act as Cairo's puppet. In this capacity he appeared in Najd with Egyptian forces

[23] Ibid. vii: 484–5.

[24] Al-Rajabī 1997: 163–4.

in 1836/37.[25] Although he installed himself in Riyadh and governed intermittently in 1837–39, the ploy did not work. Eventually, with the Egyptian forces now gone, Imam Turkī's son Fayṣal re-established himself. Bizarrely, an imposter claiming to be Khālid had arrived in Riyadh in 1832/33 and been welcomed by Imam Turkī, only to be exposed as a fraud by others who had known the real Khālid in Cairo. He was reported to have fled to Egypt and then been executed by Muḥammad 'Alī.[26]

[25] Ibn Bishr 1982–83 ii: 140.

[26] Ibid. ii: 90.

CHAPTER 10

Bowes Wright's Journey to Istanbul

From Cairo to Damascus

While the Saʻūdi imam was suffering Ottoman vengeance and others in the Wahhābi leadership were exiled or dispersed, Bowes Wright and Fisher sailed up the Nile. The former had hurried to complete his letter describing his experiences in Egypt to date for Joseph Lamb, as he left next day for Upper Egypt and did not know when he could next despatch one. He tended to pen his longest reports when his travels were stalled by adverse weather, quarantine, or the need to recuperate. On this occasion the party's plans worked out neatly, to the disadvantage of posterity.

Bowes Wright and Fisher did not envisage going far beyond Thebes, whereas Du Cane and Curteis were resolved to penetrate to the Second Cataract and even Dongola, if possible. They parted company finally at Tephe beyond Aswan. In the Valley of the Kings in Luxor (i.e. Thebes), Bowes Wright and Fisher encountered Giovanni Belzoni, living with his wife in one of the tombs. Belzoni proceeded to give them a guided tour (as Belzoni himself recorded[1]).[2] After the trip, Bowes Wright stayed in touch with him and was to witness Belzoni unrolling a mummy at the Duke of Sussex's request in March–April 1821.[3] Thereafter, both Bowes Wright and Fisher maintained their interest in Egyptology, which had a particular fascination for Freemasons because of the apparent overlap of

[1] Belzoni 1820: 372.

[2] Letter of 11 April 1819, from Damascus.

[3] Letter of 4 May 1821, from London.

symbols. In 1827, Wright wrote that Fisher had bought a very interesting mummy for him. The young Champollion, the celebrated decipherer of hieroglyphics and strong republican, whom Bowes Wright's circle admired (even if he had his English and French detractors), "has given me a charming interpretation of the handwriting on the case; it is the body of an Egyptian lady named Batro dame de la maison etc."[4]

On return to Cairo, Bowes Wright and Fisher attended a Coptic wedding and various balls, including one given by Joseph Bocty, a Syrian Christian, who acted as the Swedish consul-general and was helping Muḥammad ʿAlī create a local textile manufacturing industry. Bowes Wright, with his lively interest in ladies' appearance, observed that Miss Bocty "makes the prettiest mamaluke imaginable. Like some other frank [*sic*. Frank] ladies here she is in the habit of going out dressed à la mameluke, the male attire in a Turkish town being the convenient dress for a woman".[5] Before leaving Egypt, Bowes Wright despatched items he had acquired in the country, but most of these went missing, some lost at sea. Somewhere on this leg of his travels, he also mislaid the crest with which he sealed his letters to Joe.[6] A more serious setback was the onset during this trip of serious eye trouble, a common complaint for many foreign residents and visitors to Egypt, as well as for local inhabitants. This started to plague him badly from 1820, and its treatment caused him acute discomfort.[7] The condition seems gradually to have drained him of much of his *joie de vivre*, as he himself recognised in one of his gloomier moods when reflecting on the death of friends and loss of past pleasures.[8]

---

[4] Letter of 17 June 1827, from Paris. For Bowes Wright and Champollion, see Maitland 2015: 118–24.

[5] Letter of 11 April 1819, from Damascus. Bowes Wright tells the story of the killing of her older sister by an Albanian soldier in the street, which is also recounted by Belzoni (1820: 21) and de Forbin (1819: 290–1). The Albanian was seized by the consular janissary and, by order of the government, was secretly drowned in the Nile that night. Belzoni may have been Bowes Wright's original source on this shocking incident. See also Mengin 1823 ii: 65–7.

[6] Letter of 18 July 1820, from London.

[7] Letters of 31 March 1820, from Vienna, 27 June 1820, from Ostend, and 4 May 1821, London. Coste suffered seventeen bouts of ophthalmia during his years in Egypt (1998: 36). De Forbin reckoned that the dust in Cairo had rendered a quarter of the population completely blind (1819: 207).

[8] Letter of 27 June 1820, from Ostend.

Bowes Wright and Fisher set off from Cairo on camels with two British officers, who had once been stationed at Newcastle, to Jerusalem and then on to Damascus and Beirut. The initial journey was tough, involving sixteen days without cover or water. It was made all the harder by their translator, a Colonel Mansur, described as "a Warrant Officer of Napoleon's", deserting them and making off with many of their provisions. Now it was Bowes Wright's and his companions' turn to wear "Turkish dress à la Mamaluke, this was not necessary in Egypt, the only inconvenience there of wearing the Frank dress being that the people were afraid and fled from us; but in Syria it is very different, the people are insolent". In Damascus "it is most certain that no one could enter its gates without having his clothes torn off his back, and being otherwise ill-treated if not massacred; the Damaschini have a mortal aversion to the Hat." Yet Bowes Wright believed traditional attitudes were changing. Recent events had started to inculcate "a kind of respect for Frank prowess". One of the British officers, who spoke Arabic, told a local inhabitant of Acre governorate "in rather an Oriental way," says Bowes Wright, that "the sword of the Christian is now long, you Turks exist but by his sufferance. He fears neither your Prophet nor your Pasha."[9]

Such bravado was not in evidence when, near Jenin, the party came upon:

> the Pasha of Damascus encamped with five thousand men in the famous plains of Esdraelon, he had been eight days here and was proceeding towards Jerusalem. The scene was grand and Oriental, the camp extended from the skirts of the Samarian mount to the plain, the gilded pavilion of his Highness stood in the centre, about five hundred camels were ranged in a circular line on one side, and a little beyond were the tents of the Cajia Bey [*Kiḥyā* Bey] and the other principal officers. The rest of the ground was covered with tents and men and horses. We were received by the Pasha with the most distinguished attention, as being English and bearing the letters of Mohammed Ali of Egypt his friend and near ally. He immediately ordered us a magnificent tent for the night and shortly afterwards had us presented to him.[10]

---

[9] Letter of 11 April 1819, from Damascus.

[10] Ibid.

By this time, the usually uncomplaining Bowes Wright was starting to weary of some aspects of his expedition into the Ottoman world. Equating his own culture with 'civilization', he told Joe:

> Notwithstanding all the novel and surprising things we have seen, I begin to tire of a country where travelling is attended with so many *désagrémens* [*sic* ; *désagréments*], where the evening, the most charming part of the day in Christendom, is solitary and dull, for in a Turkish town there is no theatre, no amusement, no one thinks of stirring out at night, no creature is to be met with but ferocious dogs, but above all I am tired of a country where lovely woman is forbidden to shew her face; and I shall be delighted to find myself once more in civilised Europe.[11]

The Fellow of Jesus College readily endured hardships for the sake of new experiences and discoveries, but he was also sociable and culturally active and found the constraints and containment imposed by Ottoman customs frustrating and wearisome. Unlike so many explorers of his era, such as Burckhardt, he was not a solitary and self-contained individual, and he enjoyed varied, especially female, company. He may have been an intrepid traveller, but he was also an enthusiastic boulevardier, and that side of him was now pining for Europe.

Istanbul during the plague

From Beirut the party sailed via Cyprus along the coast of Turkey to Rhodes, Chios, and Athens. After spending time in Athens, Bowes Wright was highly derogatory about one of Ambassador Liston's predecessors in Istanbul. Describing the Acropolis, he later told Joe that "every stranger who views this sublime ruin execrates the Pictish plunderer, Lord Elgin, and 'curses the hour when from his isle he roved', thus wantonly to destroy the most delicate and best preserved ornaments of this matchless fabric".[12] After touring the Peloponnese, Bowes Wright and Fisher travelled up to unhealthy Salonica, where Sharīf Ghālib had died three years before, and embarked for the Dardanelles. Fisher was sick in Larissa and Salonica. A

[11] Ibid.

[12] Letter of 6 November 1819, from Trieste.

sad feature of Bowes Wright's travelogue in Greece and his later overland journey from Volos to Ioannina to call on 'Alī Pasha, for whom he carried a letter from Liston,[13] is the number of British travellers he met, or knew of, who fell ill and died there, often alone and in remote spots.

Bowes Wright and Fisher reached Istanbul in September 1819. Bowes Wright secured an introduction and recommendation to Liston through his British Freemasonry contacts. The Rev. G.A. Browne wrote on his behalf to William Hamilton (d. 1859), Under-Secretary at the Foreign Office (1809–22) and a Freemason, who in turn wrote to Liston about Bowes Wright.[14] The latter was impressed by the warmth of his reception: "I never in my life received more kindness and attention than from the Ambassador and Lady Liston." Liston would have been intrigued to learn of Bowes Wright's experiences in Egypt and Syria and to hear his impressions of Muḥammad 'Alī.

Bowes Wright had considered himself fortunate to have left Egypt when he did because by the spring the plague was raging at Damietta and Alexandria. He heard it had then appeared in Cairo. "We got out of Egypt in time," he noted.[15] But he and a rather reluctant Fisher, who was later to fall ill again in Smyrna, arrived in Istanbul while it was still sweeping through the city, including in Pera where it was especially bad. Liston, a highly experienced operator who had served as British envoy in Washington 1796–1800, was the only diplomat to keep his house open "with a hospitality bordering on rashness" (in Bowes Wright's view).[16] The plague had similarly affected de Forbin's stay a year before.[17] Quarantines were not in force in Istanbul, as they were increasingly elsewhere in the empire. In the jaded view of one local British doctor, this was not just because of the size of the capital's population and the ineffectiveness of the police, but because the sultan "inherits a large proportion of the

---

13 Letter of 9 September 1819, from Constantinople.

14 Ibid.; Hogg 2012: 54. Hamilton also wrote to Lord (Charles) Stewart, ambassador in Vienna and Lord Castlereagh's wild and extravagant half-brother, in the same vein (letter of 5 January 1820, from Vienna). I have not been able to establish whether Liston or Stewart were Freemasons. Hamilton was an antiquarian and Egyptologist.

15 Letter of 11 April 1819, from Damascus.

16 Letter of 9 September, from Constantinople.

17 De Forbin's visit is described in 1819: 40–8.

property of every man that dies; when all the members of a family are carried off by the plague, he inherits the whole of their property."[18]

Muḥammad 'Alī had learnt to take quarantines seriously. In December 1812, doctors had advised the pasha to impose a Western-style forty-day quarantine on vessels arriving in Alexandria from Istanbul. The plague had still ravaged the port city. Controversially, on 15 April 1813, with the plague now arrived in Cairo, the pasha ordered one in al-Gīza. This was viewed locally as a Western innovation, but the *qāḍī* investigated the claims of "the French doctor and other Greek Orthodox Christians" that this would prevent spread of the plague, and accepted their arguments. Al-Jabartī suggested, unkindly, that Muḥammad 'Alī Pasha and his regime endorsed this approach only because of their love of life and fear of death.[19] The Wahhābi reaction to the plague, when it afflicted the Sa'ūdis at the height of their regional power and influence, was more traditional. It swept through Najd in late 1808 and stalked al-Dir'iyya until July or August 1809, killing up to thirty or forty a day at its height, including a head of the religious establishment and many other notables. Imam Sa'ūd gave prayers and issued guidance to the community to be read out in mosques. He warned the people that disasters required them to turn away from sin and repent. Once this was read out in al-Dir'iyya, the plague allegedly abated.[20]

The British traveller Thomas Legh MP observed the impact of the quarantine in Egypt, although the pasha had trouble enforcing it through his Albanian troops, who initially socialised with those in quarantine.[21] The pasha was certainly keen to isolate himself from infection, irrespective of the cost of some of his measures. While the plague was moving ferociously through Cairo, he retreated from al-Azbakiyya to the palace in al-Gīza:

> with which place he would allow no communication. So strict were his orders, that any boat attempting to pass on the western side of the Nile, and consequently near his residence, was fired upon.

---

[18] MacMichael 1819: 175.

[19] Al-Jabartī 1958–67 vii: 218.

[20] Ibn Bishr 1982–83 i: 299–300.

[21] Legh 1816: 130–1; MacMichael 1819: 171–2. For a spell, Legh and MacMichael were travelling companions. MacMichael described himself as "one of Dr, Radcliffe's Travelling Fellows from the University of Oxford".

> The other side of the river was so shallow as not to be navigable; there was therefore at this point a complete interruption of all intercourse between the Delta and Upper Egypt.[22]

One notable victim of the plague in Cairo was the pasha's Italian doctor, Mandrici.[23]

Later, Legh compared his personal encounters with countries' measures against the plague in the Mediterranean with his experience of border procedures on his return home. He described "the utility and sufficiency of the usual quarantine regulations established in the countries of the Mediterranean.... But on our return to England, it was impossible not to smile at the insufficiency, not to say absurdity, of the system adopted in this country." The officer of the Board of Health insisted on presenting the captain of the vessel with a bible on which to swear the answers to their questions.:

> It was in vain we represented to him, that his taking the book again from our hands would be the surest means of communicating to him whatever infection we might ourselves be labouring under; he persisted in demanding our compliance with a form which could not be dispensed with, and added, with an air of triumph, that in the discharge of his duty, he had himself been on board several plague ships, with impunity.[24]

Such complacency and self-satisfaction were all the more surprising since periodic epidemics afflicted England too at this period. In early 1815, for example, Bowes Wright remarked on "a dreadful fever" raging across Cambridge, and "especially in Jesus College", killing staff and undergraduates. He had been due to visit the college on his retreat from a turbulent France, but wisely kept away.[25]

Although Bowes Wright and Fisher had moved bravely about Istanbul doing extensive sightseeing, the plague, which generally carried off its victims within twenty-four hours, made them curtail their visit. On 9

---

[22] Legh 1816: 130. See also al-Jabartī 1958–67 vii: 219.

[23] Ridley (n.d.): 59.

[24] Legh 1816: 139.

[25] Letter of 22 March 1815, from London.

September, at the end of his short stay there, and perhaps rarely more conscious of the fragility of life, Bowes Wright sailed on board a British government brig that was free from infection. Starting a long journey home that took him to Smyrna, Volos, overland to Ioannina, Corfu and then Trieste and Vienna, he commented: "Never shall I forget the beauty of the parting scene as the vessel fell down with the stream past the walls of the Seraglio. I think it was the finest thing I ever saw."[26] His appreciation was doubtless sharpened by relief at escaping "safe and well … from the terrible scenes of contagion and death we had witnessed in Constantinople".[27] In the circumstances, it would be understandable if he spared no thought for Sa'ūdi Imam 'Abd Allāh, who had met his death by beheading outside the Seraglio. The English Whig, whose life had intersected with that of the doomed Wahhābi leader for just an hour or two on that late autumn day in Cairo ten months before, makes no further mention of his fate in his letters.[28]

[26] Letter of 6 November 1819, from Trieste.

[27] Letter of 31 March 1820, from Vienna.

[28] Letters of 9 September 1819, from Constantinople, and of 6 November 1819, from Trieste.

CHAPTER 11

Conclusion

Even if the memory of Imam 'Abd Allāh's end was to be short-lived, his fleeting, well-publicised passage through Cairo and his presentation to the people on the streets of Istanbul before decapitation were important political theatre for both Muḥammad 'Alī Pasha and his nominal sovereign, the sultan. Bowes Wright and his companions were privileged to be in both the public and the private audience for this celebration of victory in Cairo. He understood well the episode's significance and was meticulous in recording his impressions. It is only a pity that, thanks to his imminent departure up-country, the pressure of time meant he deprived future readers of his correspondence of more valuable descriptive detail.

Both pasha and sultan aimed to exploit hard-won military success to strengthen their domestic standing. The pasha wanted to demonstrate to Cairenes that their heavy sacrifice had helped seal a gruelling expeditionary campaign with victory, and to strengthen his position in relation to Sultan Maḥmūd. The latter was eager to show the world that execution by the Seraglio was the fate marked out for those who challenged Ottoman religious credentials or invaded Ottoman dominions. The execution of Imam 'Abd Allāh was especially sweet for him because of the damage inflicted by the Wahhābis on the Ottomans' religious standing. The sacrilegious despoliation of the Prophet's tomb, as the Ottomans saw the event, had symbolised Wahhābi denial and defiance of the Ottoman religious and political heritage in the Hijaz. The sultan was determined to restore this. It proved not to be an objective so easily achieved on the ground.

Even aside from the pasha's obstructive regional ambitions, which were to develop over time into outright rebellion, there was the threat of Wahhābi resurgence. The Russian ambassador in Istanbul commented presciently in 1818 that "the defeat of the Wahhabis cannot be considered decisive".[1] Although determined to make an example of the Saʿūdi leader, Sultan Maḥmūd himself did not suppose that eradicating the Wahhābis' state would eliminate their movement. Unlike the pasha, he had no interest in the longer-term occupation of Central Arabia by Ottoman forces, nor in the further extension of Ottoman control into the fastness of Najd. His focus was on the Holy Cities and he wanted Ibrāhīm to retire to al-Madīna after securing al-Dirʿiyya.[2]

Unwilling to be constrained by his suzerain and wary of being caught in a never-ending counter-insurgency campaign, the pasha told the sultan that capture of the Wahhābi capital would not eradicate the threat to the Holy Cities, unless surviving Wahhābi elements were pursued throughout Arabia and destroyed. The sultan, who had a low opinion of Arabs and Najd, did not rate highly the chances of Ibrāhīm uprooting Wahhābism there, since it had been their creed for so long. Yet he found it hard to gainsay the pasha, to whom he was beholden for a historic victory of vital importance to him.[3]

The sultan probably underestimated the transformative impact of Muḥammad ʿAlī's campaign on the religious and ideological character of the Wahhābi movement. Contemporary and later Wahhābis were haunted by the destruction of their regime of godliness and the execution of their leader by the unbelieving Ottomans. They could not easily or comfortably explain this devastating outcome for a movement that was supposed to have God on its side. Plagued by the question of what this signified for the truth of Wahhābi doctrines, they blamed the 'sins' of the people. Ibn Bishr suggests that these sins, and the fact that all states eventually fade, accounted for the uphill battle faced by Imam ʿAbd Allāh from the time of his accession.[4] The chroniclers also highlight the speed

---

[1] Rodionov 2008: 18

[2] See e.g. letter of Maḥmūd Darwīsh to Muḥammad ʿAlī of 19 February 1819 in ʿAbd al-Raḥīm 1983: 686–7, which repeats the instruction several times.

[3] Cevdet 1874 xi: 58.

[4] 1982–83 i: 365. See also ibid. i: 277.

with which the Wahhābi system disintegrated, as Najdi turned on Najdi, and murder, robbery, and neglect of religious duties became widespread where once the regime of godliness had prevailed.[5] The Sa'ūdi state and the Wahhābi regime of godliness proved to be more fragile than most observers, and even the Wahhābis themselves, had supposed.

Despite Muḥammad 'Alī's thorough efforts to eliminate or exile its political and religious leadership, the movement duly revived in Najd in the 1820s with its capital at Riyadh, but it was to be a shadow of its former self and to remain mostly confined to the centre of Arabia until the early 20th century. The next generation of Wahhābis restored the regime of godliness, but within more confined borders and with their doctrines modified or toned down in deference to new realities. This new incarnation of the Sa'ūdi state was less aggressive and uncompromising than the first, and less effective. It was torn apart by a futile civil war between rival Āl Sa'ūd claimants to the imamate, and by the late 19th century was open to dismantlement by external enemies. Over the preceding seventy years of often precarious existence, it had exerted considerably less political and ideological influence beyond Central Arabia than its predecessor. It was as if the experiences of the final years of the First Sa'ūdi State had destroyed the self-belief and ambition of the Wahhābi movement. It did not have the same sense or spirit of manifest destiny. It became provincial and introverted, concerned more with self-preservation than the wider renewal of Islam. The war against the Ottomans, the destruction of the state, and intermittent resistance to the occupying Egyptian forces had imposed such costs that even strong Wahhābis were unprepared to risk history repeating itself.

Against the background of this trauma, it is understandable that historians have relegated the last phase of 'Abd Allāh ibn Sa'ūd's life to a footnote. By casting new light on the doomed imam's transit through Cairo, John Bowes Wright's account helps to restore this episode – and the tragic figure at its centre – to their proper place in any account of the end of the First Sa'ūdi State.

[5] Al-Fākhirī 1999: 182; Ibn Bishr 1982–83 i: 425–7. See also ibid. ii: 17.

Appendices

A. John Bowes Wright's letter of 18 November 1818 from Cairo

Grand Cairo
Nov. 18, 1818

To Joseph Lamb. Esq.
Newcastle upon Tyne.
Northumberland, England

Dear Joe,

My letter from Malta would inform you of our new dispositions with respect to Africa. We arrived off the coast of Egypt in 13 days from that island, after rather a tempestuous passage. By a mistake in calculating the Longitude, we made the land at Rosetta and were as near as possible going ashore, being only about three miles from a large ship which we saw stranded and her masts go by the board; and what is extraordinary, we afterwards found it was a vessel which we should inevitably have gone in, had we not been detained by our long passage from Naples to Malta. By a fortunate change of wind we escaped the danger and came safety to anchor in Aboukir Bay in the very place where the French fleet was attacked and destroyed by Nelson in 1798. During the two or three days we remained here we amused ourselves with examining the Fields of Battle of the 8th and 13th March [1801] when our troops first landed in Egypt. The strand is yet covered with the bones of men and horses that perished on those memorable days. Against the long wall of a French battery a tribe of Bedouin Arabs was encamped with all their camels and equipage; whilst all along to the sandy Isthmus that runs from Aboukir to Alexandria we saw groves of palm trees filled with delicious ripe fruit and guarded by other Arabs who had fixed their habitations under their shade. All this part of the country including the field of battle we found abounding in quails, against which we carried on a contest though not quite so sanguinary as had once been witnessed in these plains.

The old Saracenic Castle of Aboukir still remains pierced with shot holes and nearly a ruin. The Turks never repair anything. They were however extremely civil to us, treated us with coffee and allowed us to make signals to the ship, when we wished a boat to be sent for us. We arrived at Alexandria on the 21st. Its fine Harbour, no doubt, induced the Conqueror to build his city here, it being almost the only secure and capacious one in all this end of the Mediterranean; it certainly has no other recommendation, being surrounded on all sides by the sea or deserts of sand. On entering the city our interest was uncommonly excited by the strange and novel aspect of the various objects that presented themselves, the immense camels carrying skins of water on their backs, the Arabs cantering about on swift asses, hideous figures like women with masks upon their faces and muffled up so that only their eyes are visible, every man and boy you meet armed with a prodigious pipe, the dark face of the Ethiopian slave and the grave and pompous deportment of the Turk – these were a few of the objects we encountered on our first entrance into an Oriental town. The aspect of its interior is most miserable, and its outskirts are covered to a vast extent with ruins and excavations, the resort of myriads of unclean dogs and vultures and jackalls, which at night fill the air with their howlings.

We experienced great hospitality from Mr Lee, our Consul there, and were very much pleased by visiting the antiquities of the ancient city. It is a great pity that the Needle of Cleopatra, which has been thrown down, was not conveyed to England, as once proposed; it would have been an infinitely finer and more interesting monument than anything that will be produced by our modern architects, and under the circumstances much more appropriate.

The Needles are very similar to the larger obelisks at Rome, but are of much grander proportions, and what is more they are entire. I should tell you that in making this giro [circuit], we set out from the Consul's on asses (which are to be found ready saddled in most parts of the town) preceded by a Janizary [*sic*: Janissary], whom the Consul had assigned to us. Armed with a long white stick, he stalked majestically along, nor did he use it like our Gentleman of the White Rod, as a mere badge of office, but with heavy blows drove to the right and left asses, camels and pedestrians that in the least degree ventured to intrude upon the right line of his march. After the first novelty these scenes become painful and you behold with a feeling of sorrow the abject care-worn wretches as they steal past you; the relation of tyrant and slave is legibly written on the faces of one or other of all the Orientals I have seen. The Column called Pompey's Pillar is one of the finest I ever beheld, it is of the most highly polished granite, tho' towards the bottom it has begun to exfoliate. A barbarian designating himself T. Flinn of his B.M.S. *Tagus* has nearly covered up the whole of the antient Greek inscription by writing his classical name upon it in immense letters of black paint.[1] A Miss Talbot last year went to the top of the Pillar where 18 gentlemen were assembled at the same time. As a compliment to her enterprize they saluted her *à la ronde*, and the malicious Alexandrians say that the expected salary was one of the incitements to the undertaking. The Pillar has lately been very accurately measured, and its total height including the base and capital is 98 feet 9½ in. The plague has disappeared at Alexandria for some time, that is, there has been no case for about a month, but the fact is that town is more subject to it that any other place in the Turkish Empire; it has been particularly active these two last years, having extended into the Frank quarter, and one man having even died of the Consul's household. During the time of its prevalence the Franks shut themselves up and see no one within their houses and they sometimes remain for months in this kind of imprisonment. In the evening they mount upon their terraces, look at each other thro' glasses, and salute by signs at this distance. After visiting some Turkish Baths, which are in fact exceedingly hot vapour baths (and where the operation of rubbing and scrubbing the skin is more curious than pleasing to the eye of an European) we descended into the Cryptae or Catacombs of the ancient city. I felt considerable interest in traversing the repositories of the embalmed Egyptians, especially the circular vaulted chamber of Diana

[1] His Britannic Majesty's Ship *Tagus*, a frigate, visited Alexandria in April 1818 (Lt Col. Fitzclarence [Earl of Munster], *Journal of a Route across India, through Egypt, to England* London: John Murray, 1819: 478–9).

or Hecate and the anti-chamber leading to it. The doors of the latter are ornamented with frontispieces, having a Crescent on the pinnacle and a globe in the centre, which Clarke considered a type of the infernal sun.

We performed the journey from Alexandria to Rosetta on asses. We had not yet got our Dragoman and from the bad arrangement of our Arab conductors, who knew no other language than Arabic, we were very nearly passing the night en bivouac upon the desert. With great difficulty we contrived to reach the Chan [*sic*: Khan or inn] before midnight. The first view of Rosetta, on emerging from the desert, as seen from among the groves of palm trees that encircle it, is singularly fine; but when you enter it, like Alexandria, all is wretched and forlorn. We were enchanted with our first view of the Nile; the inundation had been greater than for these last 20 years and was still nearly at its height. We crossed to an island just opposite to the town and saw the antiquities lately sent from Thebes by Mr. Salt, and deposited there. They are principally statues of Isis and other Egyptian Deities of granite and many of them of colossal size. Nothing can be more beautiful than the vessels of the Nile when in motion, their immense sails have a perfect resemblance to a shell. The Vice-Consul having been written to we found a Dgerm in readiness to carry us to Cairo. Bailey, formerly of Trinity, and three others preceded us 2 or 3 days. The most curious sight I saw at Rosetta was a cavalcade of the ladies of the Governor's Charem [harem], each mounted on a mule and attended by a slave and guards. The Vice-Consul who was with us requested us not to look, it being contrary to Turkish manners. I however contrived to see most of them, without being cut in pieces by the sabres of the Bostangis [imperial guards, lit. gardeners]. They were all masked and covered up except the eyes which were plainly discernible and judging by these the greater part seemed neither young nor handsome; they sat astride on their mules and wore large yellow boots. The quantity of corn piled up in heaps at Rosetta along the banks of the Nile is incredible; also of chopped straw for making bricks as in the times of the ancient Israelites; and, as in those days, numerous task-masters may be seen flourishing their whips over the poor Arabs who work as porters in these corn yards. Mahommed Ali Pacha is the sole monopolizer and merchant of the corn trade and indeed of every other trade throughout the land of Egypt. He succeeded to the Pachalic on the expulsion of the Beys, and like the pasha of Joannina [Ioannina] having raised himself to power by his abilities he has made himself independent of the Porte. The banished Beys have retired to Dongola beyond the Cataracts, and Osman Bey Bardisi their chief has sworn not to shave his beard till he enters Cairo in triumph; but so firmly is the Pasha's power now established, I fear the beard of Osman will grow to more than a patriarchal length. We were ten *mortals jours* in the Dgerm between the low slimy banks of the retiring river; the information of the Belmore party respecting the Etesian [strong north] winds we found lamentably incorrect; this is not the season of their regular blowing. A strong North West wind did indeed blow the first ten days of our arrival in Egypt, and but for the cursed mistake in the Longitude which sent us into Aboukir Bay, we might have been in Cairo in 50 hours from the time of our leaving Rosetta. However we amused ourselves tolerably well during the time we passed upon the river. Whilst the Arabs were engaged in towing the Dgerm against a strong South East wind and a powerful current and, as is their custom when they work, humming a monotonous chorus, we had some excellent shooting on the banks and killed a great variety of birds unknown in Europe. At the village of Miniet-Ginadh we were present at the celebration of an Arabian marriage, and were I to detail the particulars of all the strange and obscene representations I there witnessed, I should offend as much against delicacy as I should risque [*sic*: risk] being thought by you to be narrating a traveller's story. Suffice it to say that no account I have ever read of antient or modern orgies, however licentious, is in any way comparable to what I saw that evening. Previous to this a venerable figure went round the assembled ring to collect pieces of money from such as chose to give any, as a portion for the bride. He then cried aloud the sum given and the donor's name, and the women who occupied a certain portion of the ring, made a response to each annunciation by a loud and trilling and most extraordinary cry like a high quaver in music. The sum given was generally a piaster or two, or a few paras [Ottoman coin of small value], so that when our party gave a dollar the female gratulation was more than usually shrill. The Turkish Commandant and suite who were squatted in the ring beckoned us to take places near them, and pipes and coffee were immediately served to us. These grave personages seemed to look *con amore* at the barbarous and indecent gestures of the dancers. Another strange part of the scene was the bride-groom seated on a horse just without the ring; he had already been three or four hours in that position and would have to remain there till morning, the revel continuing all night. The forming of the ring previous to the dance was by no means bad; two or three ruffians with firebrands, whips and cudgels rushed upon the crowd and drove them back with the most unsparing blows upon the head, back or limbs as it might happen. At another village (Neghidi) we saw a performance of the Almehs or dancing women; some of them wore immense rings on one of their nostrils and, like the other Egyptian women I have seen, had a blue circular mark stained upon the chin; they wear little cymbals on the finger and thumb whilst dancing and their only step is a slow measured pace; all their activity is in their derrière and that indeed is most extraordinary and indecent. After struggling for eight days with contrary winds and the rapidity of the torrent, a strong gale from the North West at last sent us rushing thro' the stream and brought us in sight of the Pyramids. These noble objects are seen at a great distance. After this we arrived at the junction of the Rosetta and Damietta branches; the undivided river is indeed a most majestic flood of water. As we approached Boulack, the Port of Cairo and about two miles from it, after dark, we perceived the most brilliant illuminations and fireworks, and when I inform you of the cause, you will I think agree with me that we could not possibly have visited this capital at a more favourable juncture, indeed I doubt if old Father Nile has witnessed such doings since the splendid days of the Pharaohs or Cleopatras [*sic*]. The Pasha had just brought an eight years' war against the Wachabites or Wehhabis to a brilliant conclusion, his son Ibrahim Pasha having taken Deraja [al-Dir'iyya] their capital and Abdallah their prince. The twenty days rejoicing at Cairo was finished, and the night of our arrival was the last but one of the seven days' Festa and grand Naumachiae [sea battles] Exhibitions at Boulack.

Next morning we observed the river covered with vessels fitted out like regular men of war and with floating Saracenic castles and temples built upon Dgerms. At noon and again before dark there was a representation of a regular attack upon the castles by the men of war which approached in full sail and under a terrible fire. The effect of such a number of cannon, the rapid movements of the ships on so famous a river as the Nile, the wide extended camp of the cavalry upon its opposite shore and the number of turbaned spectators on its margin, produced a more pleasing effect than anything I had previously witnessed. At night the ships, castles and town were illuminated, and there was a display of fireworks that would have done honor to Paris or London. I need not add that all this was under the direction of Franks, the Pasha being a liberal character, and not caring, if he be served well, whether it be by Mussulman or Christian. As his Highness was about to quit Cairo, Mr Briggs the Consul (who is also a kind of partner with the Pasha in the profits of the exportation of his corn) undertook to present us the following day at a grand Court to be held previous to his departure. As the Turks are early people we were off as soon as seven in the morning, and mounted on Arabian horses belonging to the Consulate we pranced gaily thro' "Cairo's crowded streets". Leaving the town we rode for about three miles, to the Palace of Shoubrach [Shubra], built by the Pasha upon the Nile, amidst an immense number of Mamalukes and Cavaliers splendidly dressed and mounted upon horses, asses and dromedaries. Previous to our presentation we went thro' the charem [harem] and other parts of the Palace, the females not being there. Some of the apartments are handsome and not badly painted in Arabesque. On being summoned to the Presence, we found his highness seated on the divan in one corner of the room and smoking a hooker [hookah] above 15 feet long, the Kiaja [Kihya] Bey, or Caimacan [Qa'immakam] was seated near him, all the other courtiers were standing.

After each of us had been presented, we were also placed on the Divan near his Highness; he has a fine intelligent countenance and appears to be about 55. Except the murder of the Beys, which was perhaps a matter of self-defence, I have heard him charged with no other cruelties; he has rendered his extensive territories the safest in the East to travel in; and though he monopolises the trade of the country, he has encreased its natural production in a wonderful degree. He is a most anxious encourager of arts and manufactures in Egypt, and for their better cultivation has founded a magnificent establishment in Cairo. He has extended his dominion to the cataracts on one side and over the desert to the Indian Ocean on the other having re-conquered Mecca and Medina from the Wachabites. Abdallah, the prince of that formidable sect, had just arrived a prisoner in Cairo, and was this day to have been presented to the Pasha, but for some reason this was deferred to the day following. His Highness from time to time makes a very peculiar noise with his throat which we were told was the effect of a severe cold, but which appeared to me more like the formidable and lengthened 'Aha', of our Harry 8th [Henry VIII]. During the time we were seated on the divan with him coffee was brought in to us. We were also presented to the Caimacan [Qa'immakam], Salietar [Silahdar] Bey, Ismael Pasha the son and others and above all to the celebrated Sheik Dgedid [Shadid], a powerful Bedouin Chief whose wife saved the life of Elfi Bey on his return from [missing] although he was the mortal enemy of her husband. On being informed instead of blaming her, he declared he would have struck off her head if she had betrayed or refused him the rights of Arab hospitality.

Next day was a truly interesting one; the Pasha having put off his interview with Abdallah till the afternoon, the chief interpreter had permission to introduce us to the noble Captive in a kiosque of the gardens. We found him seated on a divan with the Kiaja [Kihya] Bey and Ismael the son of the Pasha. There was a slight melancholy in his countenance but mixed with a firmness and dignity suited to his situation beyond anything I had ever witnessed. His dark visage was rather long and careworn; he wore a red shawl wrapped round his head, and a loose brown and white camlet robe, and in every respect appeared, as he was, a perfect Chief of the Desert. His grandfather was the founder of the sect. His Secretary and Treasurer were also present, two cunning wretched-looking savages.

During the interview the Pasha treated the Captive Prince with every possible attention, seating him next him on the divan, whilst even his own son and the Kiaja Bey were standing. Refreshments were served up to him and they conversed freely, thro' the interpreter on the events of the campaign. Abdallah smiled occasionally at the remarks of the Pasha; he declared he had done his utmost for the cause and that he did not repine at the lot that had been predestined him; he asked for nothing for himself, but recommended his country and family to his Highness' protection. After this to our great surprise a considerable part of the treasure was produced that had been captured by Abdallah's father at Mecca and Medina, and restored by him at the taking of his own capital Deraia [al-Dir'iyya]. These were pointed out by him one by one to the Pasha; they consisted of jewels, emeralds, the holy volumes of the Koran, set with diamonds, etc. One of the emeralds was of amazing size. After this display they were put carefully into a metallic box, double looked and sealed, and delivered into the hands of the chief courier to be conveyed to Constantinople. Abdallah accompanies him and it is generally believed will lose his head on his arrival, not only as having been so formidable a rebel to the state, but as having even threatened with absolute destruction the holy Mussulman Faith. Immediately after this ceremony the Pasha embarked in his Cangia for Damietta, his Mamloucks galloping after him along the shores of the river. We shall not be able to visit the Pyramids till our return on account of the inundation; those of Sacchara we shall see in going up. I think it very probable that we shall go no higher than Thebes, or at all events the first cataract, if the winds do not prove more favourable; as we are still anxious to reach Constantinople by March. Du Cane and Curteis are resolved to penetrate to the second cataract and perhaps to Dongola. Mr Salt, Mr Banks [*sic*; Bankes] and old Baron Sack are perhaps now in those regions. Fisher desires his remembrance to you. Give mine to Humble, Warren and my brother, the latter of whom you may apprize of my present movements. I wrote to him from Malta. You might write to me to Constantinople and get your letter sent thro' the Foreign office, to the care of our Minister there. The temperature here at present is charming, being between 60° and 70°; but the difference in heat of the morning and noonday is sometimes as much as 20°. Cairo is a large city, its numerous minarets give it a very picturesque appearance.

Yours etc,
Bowes Wright

B. Translation of al-Jabartī's account of the meeting between Muḥammad 'Alī Pasha and Imam 'Abd Allāh ibn Sa'ūd, 17 November 1818

(Al-Jabartī 1958–67 vii: 446–8)

[446] That day [Monday, 17 Muḥarram 1234 AH, equivalent to 16 November 1818 CE], 'Abd Allāh ibn Mas'ūd [*sic*; Sa'ūd] the Wahhābi arrived. He entered from the Bāb al-Naṣr [Gate of Victory], accompanied by 'Abd Allāh Baktāsh, Qubṭān of Suez. He rode a camel, flanked by the latter and preceded by a troop of light cavalry. On his entry, they fired many cannon from the citadel, Būlāq, and elsewhere. The fireworks and other displays on the banks of the Nile and Būlāq ended, and they took down the decorations. The pasha went by his vessel to Shubrā Palace and the crowd dispersed, as everyone went home. This had been one of the strangest events, unprecedented in Egypt, indeed without anything remotely comparable. The government kitchens prepared and served rice in the modern manner and [different kinds of] food for the lunch and dinner of the senior officials who had organized the displays, in addition to provisions they had from their own private kitchens and houses. The common people and the men and women celebrating went out with their children and infants onto the streets in waves and created a crush night and day on all the roads leading to Būlāq. Some were on foot, others rode. Untold sums of money were expended on these displays.

[447] On that day 'Abd Allāh the Wahhābi arrived. Then they went to the house of Ismā'īl Pasha, son of the pasha. He stayed there a day, then next morning they went with him to the pasha's in Shubrā. When he entered, he [the pasha] stood up and greeted him with a smile. He invited him to sit next to him and started talking to him. He observed that it had been a long-drawn-out affair. He ['Abd Allāh] replied that the war had had its vicissitudes. He [the pasha] asked how he had viewed Ibrāhīm Pasha. He ['Abd Allāh] said he had done his utmost and shown determination, as his own side had done, until the outcome was decreed by God. He [the pasha] said: "If God Almighty wills, I will intercede for you with our lord the sultan," to which he ['Abd Allāh] replied that what was predetermined

would come to pass. Then he [the pasha] clothed him in a cloak and he [ʿAbd Allāh] left him to go to the house of Ismāʿīl Pasha in Būlāq. The pasha boarded his boat that day and travelled in the direction of Damietta. Accompanying the Wahhābi was a small metal-covered box. The pasha asked him what it was, to which he replied: "This is what my father took from the Prophet's tomb and I am taking it with me to the sultan." So he opened it and revealed three specially commissioned Qurans, about 300 large pearls, and a large emerald with a gold cord. The pasha said to him: "Many items were taken from the tomb, not just these." ʿAbd Allāh replied: "This is what I found in my father's house. He did not take and keep everything in the tomb for himself. Senior tribesmen, the people of al-Madīna, the *āghā*s of the Ḥaram and the *sharīf* of Mecca all took pieces." The pasha said: "Correct. We found items from there with the *sharīf*."

[448] On Wednesday 19 [Muḥarram] ʿAbd Allāh ibn Masʿūd travelled in the direction of Alexandria. A troop of Tatars, as well as his personal attendants, accompanied him to *Dār al-Sulṭāna* [Istanbul].

Bibliography and Sources

Unpublished Sources

Bowes Wright Correspondence

Letters from John Bowes Wright to Joseph Lamb, held at Knighton Manor, Broadchalke, Salisbury, Wiltshire SP5 5EB, dated:

29 January 1815 from Paris

31 January 1815 from Paris

10 February 1815 from Paris

11 February 1815 from Paris

12 March 1815 from Paris

22 March 1815 from London

28 March 1815 from London

9 August 1816 from Brussels

24 May 1817 from Rome

14 July 1817 from Florence

7 March 1818 from Rome

13 May 1818 from Palermo

21 July 1818 from Naples

8 October 1818 from Malta

18 November 1818 from Grand Cairo

11 April 1819 from Damascus, with a postscript dated 25 May 1819 from Athens

9 September 1819 from Constantinople

6 November 1819 from Trieste

5 January 1820 from Vienna
31 March 1820 from Vienna
27 June 1820 from Ostend
18 July 1820 from London
4 May 1821 from London
5 June 1822 from Paris
19 February 1823, from Paris.
ca. August 1825 from Italy (incomplete)
17 June 1827 from Paris
9 June 1828 from Paris
30 July 1831, from Paris
25 January 1836 from Bowes Wright's home
Letter of William Jones in Naples to Bowes Wright of 5 April 1822
Letter of William Fisher in Paris to Bowes Wright of 5 June 1822

Other Unpublished Sources

HILL, Kara Marietta (1992), Pascal-Xavier Coste 1787–1879: A French Architect in Egypt. Unpublished PhD, MIT

IBN 'ABD AL-SHAKŪR, 'Abd Allāh ibn Muḥammad, *Tārīkh al-ashrāf.* Manuscript in the private library of Shaykh Ibrāhīm 'Aqīl at Taizz (copy lodged at the Arab League, Institute for Arabic Manuscripts, 1974)

INDIA OFFICE RECORDS (IOR), files R/15/1/14, R/15/1/19, and F/4/3441/7963 available online at https://www.qdl.qa/en/search/site/?f%255B0%255D=document_source%3Aarchive_source . Page numbers cited belong to these online files.

KING FAISAL CENTER FOR RESEARCH AND ISLAMIC STUDIES, letter of Imam 'Abd Allāh to Ṭūsūn Pasha of April/May 1815 (Collection document 00504).

LAMB, Mabel (1926), *Some Annals of the Lambs: A Border Family*. UK: privately printed (accessed online on 18.11.20 at https://archive.org/details/someannalsoflamb00lamb/page/36/mode/2up)

NATIONAL ARCHIVES, PROB 11/1894/318, item number: 3379826: will of John Bowes Wright of 13 January 1836

NORTHUMBERLAND ARCHIVES, NRO 2659/41: certificate of admission to fellowship at Jesus College, Cambridge for John Bowes Wright, 1806

Published Sources

Published Sources in Arabic

'Abd al-Ghānī, 'Ārif (1996), *Tārīkh umarā' al-Madīna al-munawwara*. Damascus: Dār Kinān lil-Ṭibā'ah wa-al-Nashr wa-l-Tawzī'

'Abd al-Raḥīm, 'Abd al-Raḥīm, ed. (1983), *Min wathā'iq al-dawla al-Sa'ūdīyya al-ūlā fī 'aṣr Muḥammad 'Alī*. Cairo: Dār al-Kitāb al-Jāmi'ī

—— (1999) *Al-Dawla al-Sa'ūdiyya al-ūlā*. Cairo: Dār al-Kitāb al-Jāmi'ī

Ajlānī, Munīr al- (1972), *Tārīkh al-bilād al-'Arabiyya al-Sa'ūdiyya, al-dawla al-Sa'ūdīyya al-ūlā, 'ahd 'Abd Allāh bin Sa'ūd*. Pt 1 (s.4). N.p.

Bassām, 'Abd Allāh Āl (1998/99), *'Ulamā' Najd khilāl thamāniya qurūn*. 2nd edition, 6 vols. Riyadh: Dār al-'Āṣima.

Bassām, Muḥammad al- (2010), *al-Durar al-mufākhir fī akhbār al-'arab al-awākhir*. 2nd edition, ed. Sa'ūd ibn Ghānim al-Jamrān al-'Ajmī. Kuwait: published privately by the editor

Daḥlān, Aḥmad ibn Zaynī (1887/88), *Khulāṣat al-kalām*. Cairo: al-Maṭba'a al-Khayriyya

Dārat al-Malik 'Abd al-'Azīz (2000), *al-Aṭlas al-tarīkhī*. Riyadh: Dārat al-Malik 'Abd al-'Azīz

Fākhirī, Muḥammad al- (1999), *Tārīkh al-Fākhirī*. Riyadh: al-Amāna al-'Āmma lil-iḥtifāl bi-murūr mi'at 'āmm 'alā tā'sīs al-mamlaka

Ḥarbī, Fā'iz al-Badrānī al- (1996), *Mudhakkirāt tārīkhīyya 'an ba'ḍ a'lām qabīlat al-Ḥarb*. 2 vols. Riyadh: Dār al-Badrānī lil-Nashr wa-l-Tawzī'

Ibn Bishr, 'Uthmān (1982–83) *'Unwān al-majd fī tārīkh Najd*. 2 vols. Riyadh: Dārat al-Malik 'Abd al-'Azīz

Ibn Ghannām, Ḥusayn (1949), *Tārīkh Najd al-musammā Rawḍat al-afkār wa-l-afhām*. 2 parts. Riyadh: al-Maktaba al-Ahliyya

Ibn Ḥumayd, Muḥammad (1989), *Al-Suḥub al-wābila 'alā ḍarā'iḥ al-Ḥanābila*. N.p.: Maktabat al-Imām Aḥmad

Ibn 'Īsā, Ibrāhīm (1999), *Tārīkh ba'ḍ al-ḥawādith al-wāqi'a fī Najd*. Riyadh: al-Amāna al-'Āmma lil-iḥtifāl bi-murūr mi'at 'āmm 'alā tā'sīs al-mamlaka

Ibn Khamīs, 'Abd Allāh (1982), *al-Dir'iyya*. Riyadh: published privately.

Ibn Qāsim, 'Abd al-Raḥmān (1996–99), *al-Durar al-saniya fī al-ajwiba al-Najdiyya*. 16 vols. N.p.

Jabartī, 'Abd al-Raḥmān al- (1958–67), *'Ajā'ib al-āthār fī tarājim wa-al-akhbār*. 7 vols. Cairo: Lajnat al-Bayān al-'Arabī

KŪRSHŪN, Zakariyā (2010), *al-'Uthmāniyyūn wa-Āl Sa'ūd fī al-arshīf al-'Uthmānī*. Beirut: al-Dār al-'Arabiyya lil-Mawsū'āt

MAKTABAT AL-MALIK 'ABD AL-'AZĪZ (2006/7), Maktabat al-Imām 'Abd Allāh ibn Sa'ūd. Riyadh: Maktabat al-Malik 'Abd al-'Azīz al-'āmma

MAWJĀNĪ, 'Alī (2014), *Wathā'iq Najd*. Beirut: Dār al-Maḥajja al-Bayḍā'

MUTAWALLĪ, Aḥmad (1991), *Āl Sa'ūd wa-l-Shām fī 'ahd al-dawla al-Sa'ūdiyya al-ulā 'alā ḍaw' al-wathā'iq al-turkiyya*. Cairo: Dār al-Zahrā' lil-Nashr

QAḤṬĀNĪ, Fāṭima al- (2010), *Ḥamlat Ibrāhīm Pāshā 'alā al-Dir'iyya wa-suqūṭuha*. Riyadh: Dārat al-Malik 'Abd al-'Azīz

QĀYĀ, Dilak (2008), *Karbalā' fī al-arshīf al-'Uthmānī*. Beirut: al-Dār al-'Arabiyya lil-Mawsū'āt

RAJABĪ, Khalīl ibn Aḥmad al- (1997), *Tārīkh al-Wazīr Muḥammad 'Alī Pāshā*. Ed. Daniel Crecelius. Cairo: Dār al-Āfāq al-'Arabiyya

RASHĪD, Amīr Ḍārī ibn Fuhayd al- (1966), *Nubdha tārīkhiyya 'an Najd*. Riyadh: Dār al-Yamāma

RIḌĀ, Rashīd ed. (1928), *Majmū'at al-rasā'il wa-l-masā'il al-Najdiyya*. 4 vols. Cairo: al-Manār

ṢĀBĀN, Suhayl (2004), *Madākhil ba'ḍ a'lām al-jazīra al-'arabiyya fī al-arshīf al-'Uthmānī*. Riyadh: Maktabat al-Malik 'Abd al-'Azīz al-'āmma

—— (2005) *Makka al-mukarrama wa-l-Madīna al-munawwara, buḥūth wa-dirāsāt min wāqi' al-arshīf al-'Uthmānī wa-l-maṣādir al-turkiyya*. Riyadh: Maktabat al-Malik 'Abd al-'Azīz al-'āmma

SHAYKH, 'Abd al-Raḥmān ibn Ḥasan Āl al- (2005), *al-Maqāmāt*. Riyadh: Dārat al-Malik 'Abd al-'Azīz

ZAYDĀN, Muḥammad (1975), Al-Wathā'iq tatakallam, *al-Dāra* 1, pp. 159–91

Published Sources in Other Languages

ABU-MANNEH, Butrus (1982), The Naqshbandiyya-Mujaddidiyya in the Ottoman Lands in the Early 19th century. *Die Welt des Islams* 22 (1), pp. 1–36

ANON. (1826), Buckingham v. Bankes (libel case). *The Oriental Herald* 11 (354) Oct.–Dec., pp. 375–460

ANON. (1833), *Cambridge University Calendar*, 1833. Cambridge: J. & J.J. Deighton

ASHMOUNI, Marwa El, and BARTSCH, Katharine (2014), Egypt's Age of Transition: Unintentional Cosmopolitanism during the Reign of Muhammad 'Alī (1805–1848), *Arab Studies Quarterly* 36 (1), pp. 43–74

BELZONI, Giovanni (1820), *Narrative of the Operations and Recent Discoveries … in Egypt and Nubia*. London: John Murray

BONACINA, Giovanni (2015), *The Wahhabis Seen though European Eyes (1772–1830)*. Leiden: Brill

BOSWORTH, C.E. (1974), Henry Salt, Consul in Egypt 1816–27 and Pioneer Egyptologist. *Bulletin of the John Rylands Library* 57, pp. 69–91

BRYDGES, Sir Harford Jones (1834), *An Account of the Transactions of His Majesty's Mission to the Court of Persia in the years 1807–11*. 2 vols. London: James Bohn

BURCKHARDT, John Lewis (1831), *Notes on the Bedouins and Wahábys*. 2 vols. London: Henry Colburn and Richard Bentley

BURDETT, A.L.P, ed. (2013) *The Expansion of Wahhabi Power in Arabia 1798–1932*. 8 vols. Cambridge: Cambridge Archive Editions

CEVDET Pasha, Ahmed (1874), *Tārīḥ-i Cevdet*. 12 vols. Istanbul: Maṭbaʿa ʿUthmāniyya

COSTE, Pascal-Xavier (1998), Les Mémoires d'un artiste en Égypte. In Dominique Jacobi, ed., *Toutes les Égyptes*, pp. 31–48. Marseille: Parenthèses

CRAWFORD, Michael (2014), *Ibn 'Abd al-Wahhab*. London: Oneworld Publications

CRAWFORD, Michael and FACEY, William (2017), ʿAbd Allāh Al Saʿūd and Muḥammad ʿAlī Pasha: The Theatre of Victory, the Prophet's Treasures, and the Visiting Whig, Cairo 1818. *Journal of Arabian Studies* 7 (1) (April 2017)

EVERED, Emine (2012), Rereading Ottoman Accounts of Wahhabism as Alternative Narratives: Ahmed Cevdet Paşa's Historical Survey of the Movement. *Comparative Studies of South Asia, Africa and the Middle East* 32 (3), pp. 622–32

FACEY, William (1992), Riyadh: *The Old City: From its Origins until the 1950s*. London: Immel Publishing

—— (1997), *Dirʿiyyah and the First Saudi State*. London: Stacey International

FAHMY, Khaled (2002), *All the Pasha's Men: Mehmed Ali, His Army and the Making of Modern Egypt*. Cairo, New York: American University in Cairo Press

FAIRHOLT, F.W. (1862), *Up the Nile, and Home Again*. London: Chapman & Hall

FORBIN, Auguste Comte de (1819), *Voyage dans le Levant en 1817 et 1818*. 2nd edition. Paris: l'Imprimerie Royale

FUSSELL, Paul (1980), *Abroad: British Literary Traveling between the Wars*. Oxford: Oxford University Press

GALTIER, Gérard (2006), La société secrète égyptienne de B. Drovetti. *Cahiers de la Méditerranée* 72 (La Franc-Maçonnerie en Méditerranée [XVIIIe – XXe siècle]), pp. 1–15

GAURY, Gerald de (1951), *Rulers of Mecca*. London: Harrap

HALLS, J.J. (1834), *The Life and Correspondence of Henry Salt*, Esq. 2 vols. London: Richard Bentley

HOGG, Bruce (2012), *Freemasons and the Royal Society: Alphabetical List of Fellows of the Royal Society who were Freemasons*. 2nd edition. Published online on behalf of the Library and Museum of Freemasonry. Accessed at https://studylib.net/doc/8838262/freemasons-and-the-royal-society-alphabetical-list-of, on 08.01.21

IRBY, Charles, and MANGLES, James (1845), *Travels in Egypt and Nubia, Syria, and the Holy Land*. London: John Murray

JASMIN, Denise (1998), Les Dessins d'Architecture Civile. In Dominique Jacobi, ed., *Toutes les Égyptes*, pp. 131–62. Marseille: Parenthèses

LANDAU, Jacob (1965), Prolegomena to a Study of Secret Societies in Modem Egypt. *Middle Eastern Studies* 1 (2), January, pp. 135–86

LEGH, Thomas (1816), *Narrative of a Journey in Egypt and the Country beyond the Cataracts*. London, John Murray

LINNEAN SOCIETY (1855), *Proceedings of the Linnean Society of London 1848–55*. 2 vols. London: Taylor and Francis

LORIMER, John (1915), *Gazetteer of the Persian Gulf, 'Omān, and Central Arabia*, 2 vols. Calcutta: Government Printing, India

MACMICHAEL, William (1819), *Journey from Moscow to Constantinople in the years 1817, 1818*. London: John Murray

MAITLAND, Margaret (2015), Hieroglyphs from the North: Newcastle's Early Travellers in Egypt and Their Correspondence with Jean-François Champollion. In Neil Cooke and Vanessa Daubney, eds., *Every Traveller Needs a Compass: Travel and Collecting in Egypt and the Near East*, pp. 113–30. Oxford: Oxbow Books

MANLEY, Deborah (1999), Letters to a Friend. *Bulletin of the Association for the Study of Travel in Egypt and the Near East* (ASTENE) 7, p. 19

MARSOT, Afaf Lutfi al-Sayyid (1984), *Egypt in the reign of Muhammad Ali*. Cambridge: Cambridge University Press

MAZOWER, Mark (2005), *Salonica, City of Ghosts*. London: Harper Perennial

MENGIN, Félix (1823), *Histoire de l'Égypte sous le gouvernement de Mohammed-Aly*. 2 vols. Paris: Arthus Bertrand

Mitchell, Leslie (2007), *The Whig World 1760–1837*. London: Hambledon Continuum

O'Quinn, Daniel, ed. (2009), *The Travels of Mirza Abu Taleb Khan*. Toronto, Broadview Press

Philipp, Thomas (2001), *Acre: The Rise and Fall of a Palestinian City 1730–1831*. NY: Columbia University Press

Pocock, Tom (2005), *Stopping Napoleon: War and Intrigue in the Mediterranean*. London: John Murray

Qasimi, Sultan Muhammad al-, ed. (1995), *The Journals of David Seton in the Gulf 1800–1809*. Exeter: University of Exeter Press

Reynolds-Ball, E.A. (1899), *Cairo of To-day*. London: Adam and Charles Black

Ridley, Ronald T. (n.d.), *Napoleon's Proconsul in Egypt: The Life and Times of Bernardino Drovetti*. London: Rubicon Press

Roberts, Andrew (2014), *Napoleon the Great*. London: Allen Lane

Rodionov, Mikhail (2008), The First and Second Saudi States. In Fahd al-Semmari, ed., *The Kingdom of Saudi Arabia in 100 Years*, pp. 7–35. Riyadh: King Abdul Aziz Foundation

Rodkey, Frederick (1933), The Attempts of Briggs and Company to Guide British Policy in the Levant in the Interest of Mehemet Ali Pasha, 1821–41. *The Journal of Modern History* 5 (3), pp. 324–51

Rottiers, Colonel Bernard (1829), *Itinéraire de Tiflis à Constantinople*. Brussels: Chez Frechet

Sadleir, G. Forster (1866), *Diary of a Journey across Arabia*. Bombay: Education Society's Press, Byculla

Sarhan, Saud al- (2016), The Saudis as Managers of the Hajj. In Eric Tagliacozzo and Shawkat M. Toorawa, eds., *The Hajj, Pilgrimage in Islam*, pp. 196–212. NYC: Cambridge University Press

Seetzen, Ulrich (1805), Fortgesetzte Reise-Nachrichten des Dr U.J. Seetzen. *Monatliche Correspondenz zur Beförderung Der Erd- und Himmels-Kunde* 12, pp. 234–41

Tagher, Jacques (1950), Un Diplomate Malchanceux: Félix Mengin. *Cahiers d'Histoire Égyptienne*, Série II (4), pp. 372–80

The Times of London, issues of 1 August 1817, and 9 January and 6 February 1819

Tugay, Emine Foat (1963), *Three Centuries: Family Chronicles of Turkey and Egypt*. London: Oxford University Press

USICK, Patricia (2002), *Adventures in Egypt and Nubia: The Travels of William John Bankes (1786–1855)*. London: British Museum Press

VASSILIEV, Alexei (1998), *The History of Saudi Arabia*. London: Saqi Books

VENN, John (1954), *Alumni Cantabrigienses: A Biographical List of All Known Students, Graduates and Holders of Office at the University of Cambridge, from the Earliest Times to 1900*. Vol. 2, pt. 6. Cambridge: Cambridge University Press

VERDERY, Richard N. (1976), The Use of al-Jabartī's *'Ajā'ib al-Āthār* by the Historian Félix Mengin. In Donald P. Little, ed., *Essays on Islamic Civilization Presented to Niyazi Berkes*, pp. 329–41. Leiden: Brill

VLAMI, Despina (2014), *Trading with the Ottomans: the Levant Company in the Middle East*. London: IB Tauris

WELFORD, Richard (1895), *Men of Mark 'Twixt Tyne and Tweed*. 3 vols. London and Newcastle-Upon-Tyne: Walter Scott Ltd

WILSON, David (2011), *List of British Consular Officials in the Ottoman Empire*, July 2011, accessed at http://www.levantineheritage.com/pdf/List_of_British_Consular_Officials_Turkey(1581-1860)-D_Wilson.pdf on 06.03.20.

WILSON, Sir Robert (1803), *A Narrative of the British Expedition to Egypt*. London: R. Dutton

WISSA, Karim (1989), Freemasonry in Egypt 1798–1921: A Study in Cultural and Political Encounters. *BRISMES Bulletin* (British Society for Middle Eastern Studies) 16 (2), pp. 143–61

ZIVIE, Alain (1998), Pascal Coste Égyptologue. In Dominique Jacobi, ed., *Toutes les Égyptes*, pp. 163–88. Marseille: Parenthèses

Index

In alphabetising, the definite article (al-) and the word Āl (meaning 'house' or 'clan') have been ignored.

Abbreviations

BW Bowes Wright
EIC East India Company
MA Muḥammad 'Alī Pasha